It's Not Rocket Science

It's Not Rocket Science

The Theology of
St. Paul The Apostle

3rd Edition ©

IRVING L. BRITTLE JR.

It's Not Rocket Science: The Theology of Saint Paul The Apostle

This book is written to provide information and motivation to readers. Its purpose is not to render any type of psychological, legal, or professional advice of any kind. The content is the sole opinion and expression of the author, and not necessarily that of the publisher.

Copyright © 2021 by Irving L Brittle Jr.

All rights reserved. No part of this book may be reproduced, transmitted, or distributed in any form by any means, including, but not limited to, recording, photocopying, or taking screenshots of parts of the book, without prior written permission from the author or the publisher. Brief quotations for noncommercial purposes, such as book reviews, permitted by Fair Use of the U.S. Copyright Law, are allowed without written permissions, as long as such quotations do not cause damage to the book's commercial value. For permissions, write to the publisher, whose address is stated below.

Printed in the United States of America.

ISBN: 978-1-956515-09-1 (Hardcover)
ISBN: 978-1-956515-08-4 (Paperback)
ISBN: 978-1-956515-07-7 (Digital)

GSH books may be ordered through booksellers, or directly from:
Global Summit House,

New York, New York
WWW.Global Summit House.com

Book Ordering Information

Phone Number: 315 288-7939 ext. 1000 or 347-901-4920
Email: info@globalsummithouse.com

To God and St. Paul the Apostle. To my wife, Sue King Brittle, my 'rock and anchor' for over 33 years. She has been my source of 'Peace and Joy' and taught me the value of 'family.'

My daughter, Ashton Leigh Freeman, with whom I live in Clermont, Florida and only child, and one who has made her parents proud.

My Grandson, Ryder Luke Freeman, whom 'keeps me on my toes, freely offering moments of laughter and enjoyment' as I learn what goes on in the minds of 'little people' and their worlds.

My parents, Helen P. Brittle and Irving L. Brittle, whom raised me with my two sisters teaching us the values of 'hard work that has its rewards;' sacrificing, with God's guidance, to give us 'a life,' now looking back, full of a blessed home life.

My New 'Brothers and Sisters in The Body of Christ' at First Baptist Clermont, Clermont, Florida

Dr. Charles F. Stanley and "The Life Principles Bible"

Contents

Preface & Brief thoughts ix

Paul's Early Life Historical Summation... 1
Who Were the Pharisees?... 4
Paul, A Zealot Pharisee.. 7
St. Paul & the Damascus Road.. 10
The Way, Christianity A New Beginning.. 14
God and Mankind 18
The Law and The Term 'Adam' The Dark Side of Humanity....24
Sin and The Law 29
A New Gospel, "*The Way*," and A Way to Holiness.................. 34
FINALLY, You're a Christian 'Walking the Walk' - Pathways....37
Baptism... 45
Righteousness... 48
Justification 50
You've Been Justified Complete with the Benefits and Work
    Ahead of You 53
Sanctification and Salvation 60
- Principal 1: The Need to Know (Romans 6:3-5) 63
- Principle 2: Consider Yourself Dead 66
- Principle 3: Present Yourself to God (Romans 6:13) 67

The Lord's Supper 72
Martin Luther – A Fresh Look at the Old Doctrine of
    Justification by Faith.. 78
The Fruit of the spirit... 82
Words & Definitions.. 85

Bibliography.. 87

Preface & Brief thoughts

Having studied and attempting to comprehend the theology of St. Paul the Apostle, I have come to realize *the theology of Christianity is not rocket science* per St. Paul. As St. Paul expounded through his epistles, it is *a personal relationship and faith in one living God through His Son, Jesus Christ.*

Have you been questioned, or challenged to debate your Christian beliefs and values? I have! In the current times in which we live in America, Christianity has come under attack - more and more. Some believe we are living in a 'Godless nation;'[1] many do not believe in a living God, or Jesus Christ. How did this movement come into being, and how did we get to this point!?

Jesus Christ and St. Paul lived over two-thousand years ago in a time when Rome ruled most of the *civilized* world, and many pagan religions ran rampant. The Romans and Greeks believed in 'gods and goddesses' in humanlike form that populated an invisible realm who were distinguished from mere mortals only by their perceived powers and immortality.

These were gods of arbitrary pleasure with no morality whatsoever. Their traits exhibited greed, sensuality, and jealous thievery. Most were vindictive scoundrels. The stories surrounding the gods did *not* lift the heart or calm the anxiety of mystery, nor did they inspire a desire to be good or moral.

The ancient civilizations were content to offer purely formalistic worship to the hidden powers that moved the world, provided the ceremonies were conducted with the prescribed pomp and pageantry. The pagan religions were protected and supported by the state and local officials that decided which gods would be

---

[1] America… A Godless Nation,' *Salvation in Jesus Ministry,* www.sijministry, YouTube, October 27, 2014.

venerated and to whom sacrifices could be offered.

The idea of true religious piety was foreign (as *Christians* may know today) to the minds and souls of the many people living in the Roman Empire. Nothing remained but empty idolatrous cults, superstition rituals, and magic, none of which satisfied the desire for an assurance of happiness. Pessimism reigned. Uneasiness therefore tormented souls. But there were men and women who did seek salvation in a new theology and religion called '*The Way*' centered in Jesus Christ, the Son of God, the Messiah and Savior.

There were leaders, especially in Rome who adopted the title of 'savior;' a title given to many ancient and newer divinities who desired to be shielded from the threats of life and death. In the outlying areas of the empire there were those who participated in other mystery religions associated with the oriental cults, including cults such as Attis and Cybele in Asia Minor, and Osiris and Isis in Egypt.

Issues in these religions scarcely touched on or included the concepts of sin and the idea of purity of the soul. The Greeks, Romans *and Jews* living in the empire, did understand the concept of purity in reference to bathing, food and fasting, but the idea of inner moral purity (purity of the soul) was a foreign concept.[2]

The beginning of the of the Christian era was a great age of spiritual and religious awakening, a quest for truth, and a search for the one true God. One of the God-seekers, the greatest among them next to Jesus Christ, was Paul of Tarsus. "He became the instrument chosen directly by the one true God to preach a universal religion in a common language, throughout an empire unified under the aegis of Rome."[3]

St. Paul has become a Christian mentor, and in a sense, long-ago friend. His theology can be made complicated, controversial, and hard to comprehend and understand depending on the *many*

---

[2] Irving L. Brittle Jr, *St Paul the Apostle: The Right Man at the Right Time, Third Edition* (Pen House LLC, 2020), 8,9.

[3] Joseph M. Callewaert, *The World of St. Paul,* trans. Michael J. Miller (San Francisco: Ignatius Press, 2011), 18.

authors, theologians, or researchers you decide to read and explore first. I have studied, researched and *condensed* information from more than seventy sources on the topic of St. Paul and his theology. With a degree of confidence, I can say there are numerous opinions on St. Paul the man and as many, or more opinions on his theology. I believe I have a relatively good sense of St. Paul, the man and his theology – *it's not rocket science.*

God and Jesus Christ chose, and appointed Paul,[4] to deliver the crux of Christian theology, *'The Way,'* to *'all mankind,'* and Paul believed Jesus Christ was the true, long awaited Messiah, and Son of God. As the title reads from my first book, **St. Paul The Apostle: The Right Man at the Right Time**, he was the perfect man to set this new idea, theology and religion in motion.

St. Paul was a man of obvious intelligence and genius. He would never take the credit for his intelligence or the truths and philosophies in the messages of his epistles – they were God given.[5] Paul came to believe all gifts are given freely from God the Father, including intelligence and intellect. "Thanks be to God for His indescribable gift!"[6]

> 'During Paul's life, God continued to be the bedrock and foundation of his theology. He never ceased to maintain the first two commandments of the Decalogue – to have no other gods besides the one True God, and to abhor idolatry with all his soul.'[7]

---

[4] Dr. Charles f. Stanley, *Life Principles Bible* (La Habra, CA: The Lockman Foundation, 2009), Acts 9: 5-7.
[5] Ibid. Galatians 1: 11,12.
[6] Ibid. 2 Corinthians 9:15.
[7] James D. G. Dunn, *The Theology of St. Paul the Apostle* (Grand Rapids, MI: William Be Eerdman's Publishing Company, 1998), 717.

Paul's Early Life Historical Summation

As noted in *St. Paul: The Right Man at the Right Time*, Paul and his family lived in the city of Tarsus in Cilicia (modern day Turkey). Tarsus was known for what we may call today a college/university town as many noted philosophers, teachers, and scientists resided within its city limits. It was also a city known for its fine textiles.

Paul grew up and was raised in a fundamentalist Jewish family, and *he was Hebrew*.[8] Paul's family were Diaspora Jews (Jews not living in the Holy Land) and were *Roman citizens* with all the perks bundled into that designation.

The family recited their morning and evening prayers (*the Shema*) while facing Jerusalem and attended their synagogue each week. Paul's mother raised her young son until the age of six; then Paul's father took over. Paul became, by trade, a tent maker later in his youth following in his father's footsteps (Paul's father may have also been a Pharisee. Acts 23:6 quotes Paul referring to his father by saying "he, Paul was a Pharisee, the son of a Pharisee[s]…").[9]

At his youngest school age Paul attended a local synagogue school called a *vineyard*. (Jewish parents believed their children should be 'nourished and pruned' like the vines of a vineyard). It was basic schooling – reading and writing mostly in the sand, but occasionally on a piece of papyrus. The lessons were repetitive, possibly mind numbing, and rhetorical. That was the schooling method of the times, and obviously, that method proved perfect and effective for Paul.

At age thirteen, Paul participated in his *bar mitzvah* and had the opportunity to stand before his synagogue and declare, "Today, I am a man." At this time also Paul formally started an

---

[8] Stanley, *Life Principles Bible*, Acts 21:39, 22:3.
[9] En.wikipedia.org/Paul_the_Apostle, Biblical narrative, Early life, accessed October 1, 2019.

apprenticeship in his father's trade and helping earn family income – that being a tentmaker (tents during Biblical times were made of leather or goat skin and woven hairs. Tarsus was famous for their goat skin shelters). During his missions, Paul did not rely on his 'followers or new believers' for handouts, or money. He 'earned a living' as a tentmaker wherever he lived for extended periods as well as building churches and bringing new believers to Christ. (see 2 Thessalonians 3:10).[10]

Between the age of 14-to-16, Paul left for Jerusalem and entered the school of the Pharisees headed by *Gamaliel*. Gamaliel was an esteemed Pharisee and eminent 'doctor' of the Jewish law. Gamaliel was the grandson of Hillel, and first of seven rabbis to earn the title of Rabban.[11]

At the school of Gamaliel, students learned the history of the Jewish people, as well as their sense of values, tenets and laws of Moses – **the Torah**. In class, there were questions and answers constantly tossed about concerning certain aspects of the laws. The rabbis (teachers) challenged their students, and the students '*were allowed*' to challenge the rabbis. There unquestionably were massive amounts of memory work concerning the Jewish Laws (613 total). The students were required to learn their studies by heart.

Paul proved himself to be an excellent student and scholar. While at the school of Gamaliel, Paul also became acquainted with the Greek culture, Greek writings and dialect. During his later missions he could present the gospel in either Hebrew, Aramaic, or Greek, and it was noted he spoke Greek with authority and purity of dialect, not as one who had to learn it at a late age. Paul was exposed and felt comfortable with the Greek language, his Greek and Jewish classmates, friends and later, the Gentile followers and believers of '*the Way.*'

---

[10] Stanley, 2 Thessalonians 3:10.
[11] Ibid. Acts 22:3.

Paul knew when he completed his degree as rabbi, he was more aptly equipped to be a rabbi, and teach the Torah than others. "I progressed in Judaism beyond many of my contemporaries among the people, being exceedingly zealous for my ancestral traditions."[12] Paul would be a Pharisee of noted intensity and zeal – *a Zealot.*

---

[12] Ibid. Galatians 1:14.

Who Were the Pharisees?

Who *exactly* were the Pharisees? The Pharisees were one of three prominent 'parties,' and/or leadership sects of Judaism, and they by far were the most influential among the Jewish people. The name *Pharisee,* which in its Semitic form means *the separated ones, separatist,* first appeared during the reign of John Hyrcanus (135BC).[13]

Three facets of the Jewish nation contributed to the development of the Pharisees, or paradoxically, it may be said that the Pharisees *made these contributions* to Judaism so, ultimately the terms *Pharisee* and *Judaism* became almost synonymous:

- The first characteristic was *Jewish legalism* that began in earnest after the Babylonian captivity (approximately 540 BC). Temple worship and sacrifices had ceased, and Judaism began to center its activities in Jewish Law and the synagogues.

- The rise of the *Jewish scribes,* who were closely associated with the Pharisees, gave great impetus to Jewish legalism. The Pharisees were more of a 'fraternal order' or religious society than a sect and were the organized followers of these experts (the scribes) in interpreting the scriptures. They formalized the religion of the scribes and put it into practice. The Pharisees were religious leaders of the Jews, not so much 'practical politicians' which is attributed to the more liberal Sadducees,

---

[13] J. D. Douglas and Merrill C. Tenney, *NIV Compact Dictionary of the Bible* (Grand Rapids, MI: Zondervan Publishing, 1989), p.453.

- A second characteristic was Jewish *nationalism*. Continued persecution and isolation of the Jews crystallized this spirit. During the Babylonian captivity the Jews were a small minority in a foreign nation. The fierce persecution of the Jewish people by Antiochus Epiphanes (175-164 BC) was a bold attempt to Hellenize and assimilate the Jews, but that only drew the Jewish people closer together. The Pharisees took that occasion to cultivate a national and religious consciousness that has hardly been equaled and continues to this day,

- The third contributing factor of Pharisaism was the development and organization of the Jewish religion *itself* after the Babylonian captivity and Maccabean Revolt (167- 160 BCE).[14] Included was the formulation and adaptation of Mosaic law by scribes and rabbis, increased tradition, and *extreme separatism* slowly helped generate a new religion vehemently opposing all secularization of Judaism by the pagan Greek thought that penetrated Jewish life after the Alexandrian conquest - this occurred in 329 BCE (it's interesting to note that Alexander the Great, a Greek, was *not* a pagan; he believed "*one God existed*, the *God of Cause*" which is important as it helped explain why Alexander was able to tolerate beliefs of the Jewish people and their religion').[15] The Pharisees became a closely organized group that pledged themselves to obey all facets of the Jewish traditions down to the *minutest details* and were sticklers for ceremonial purity.

The doctrines of the Pharisees included the following:
- Predestination,
- The immortality of the soul,
- Belief in spirit life

---

[14] *Maccabean Revolt*- Wikipedia, en.wikipedia.org/wiki/Maccabean Revolt.
[15] *Alexander the Great*. www.jewishhistory.org/alexander-the great.

They believed in a final reward for good works, and souls of the wicked were detained forever under the earth in the abode for the dead named *Sheol* (hell), while those of the virtuous rose again and even migrated into other bodies. They accepted the Old Testament scriptures and fostered the usual Jewish messianic hope which they gave a material and nationalistic twist.

Paul, A Zealot Pharisee

Paul *was* a Pharisee and was *'zealous'* in executing his duties as a Pharisee. He persecuted those who aligned themselves with a new religion and belief known initially as *'The Way'* – the followers and believers of Jesus Christ, the Messiah and Savior. He literally went door to door seeking the followers of *the Way*, incarcerating whole families and for some unfortunate believers, having them put to death.[16] [17]

An additional reason to explore the subject of Paul's education and Paul as a zealous Pharisee is to inform readers how Paul dealt with his learned Judaic religion as *he knew, and fervently believed in his time* up to his conversion/transformation on the Damascus road.

Paul was a proud Jew. He would never state it in that context. What he advocated after his Damascus road encounter with Christ, he called a *'new and true Judaism;' this experience* making the first version obsolete. He maintained the Torah had been superseded by the *new Torah of Christ*.[18]

After Paul's Damascus road experience (which is the subject of the next chapter), he did transform his belief system and focused on the Spirit of God and Jesus Christ, but he never distanced himself from all Mosaic Laws and many Jewish traditions. Some say Paul turned his back on the Torah's revelations given to Moses with its laws, customs and traditions with a new focus on the *Torah of Christ*[19]- *not true!* Now, even though his thoughts were more centered in *Christology*, he knew the words and laws given to Moses were *'God given.'* One of Paul's arguments concerning

---

[16] Stanley, *Life Principles Bible,* Gal. 1:13.
[17] Ibid. 1 Kings 19:10.
[18] Ibid. Philippians 3:4-8.
[19] James D. Tabor, *Paul and Jesus* (New York: Simon and Schuster, 2012), p. 16.

the apparent dichotomy of his new situation was 'the Law and the Ten Commandments given to Moses *were* given by God, and that made them inherently holy.'[20] Possibly having abandoned some of his earlier Judaism, Paul *never* became anti-Semitic.

Paul's transformation from a zealous Pharisee to the leading figure and proponent of *the Way*, was fraught with new obstacles and danger for him personally. He still lived amongst his fellow Jews (including Judaizers, Pharisees and Sadducees) who countered and *'adamantly' did not believe* in *the Way* and saw it as a threat to Judaism *and blasphemous*. His new theology concerning Christ could have led to *his* execution and almost did on several occasions throughout the remainder of his life.

With his new Christology, Paul, from the first epistle possibly to the Galatians or the Thessalonians, to the last Pastoral Epistles, grew in understanding the phrase *living in Christ Jesus,* and it showed in the maturity of his thoughts and writings over time. As his faith grew, Paul's evangelism and writings got stronger and better. He used many metaphors and parallelisms in his evangelism and in scripture. Paul did not try to make his theology inherently difficult; it was simply the way his brilliant mind thought and evangelized in words and speech. A new journey now begins into *the "multifaceted mind"*[21] of St. Paul the Apostle and his theology. I encourage you while reading alone, or in group settings, *to stop, look and listen* and question what you believe is the point of the material presented. If there is any consolation - philosophers, theologians, historians, Sunday school teachers now, and through the ages still debate what Paul's theology is, and how it may have been presented to new believers during his time.

We are reading and studying a religious theology that took root over two thousand years ago, and *some* before the earliest books of the Old and New Testament. One conclusion in our modern era is, 'things really haven't changed that much.' Christianity is a religion,

---

[20] Stanley, *Life Principles Bible*, Galatians 3:23-26.
[21] Thomas D. Lea and David Alan Black, *The New Testament: It's Background and Message* (Nashville, TN: B & H Publishing Group, 2003), p.345.

and once the *'incarnate personage'* of Christ, the cornerstone of Christianity, entered the world, the history of Christianity as a whole, began.

> *'For Paul, "Christianity is Christ." It is not only in the clarification and sharper definition of his heritage that the centrality of Christ for Paul's theology is evident. Christ is the thread which runs through all, the lens through which all comes to focus, the glue which bonds the parts into a coherent whole.*[22]

---

[22] Dunn, *The Theology of Paul the Apostle*, p.724.

St. Paul & the Damascus Road

Our continuing journey into the theology of St. Paul will start with his trip on the road to the city of Damascus, now in modern day Syria. His mission was to, again root out and prosecute as many of the followers of *the Way* as he could find. He was to *'bind and shackle'* them and return to Jerusalem.[23]

He laid waste to the followers of *the Way* in Jerusalem and was looking for new territory and *'believers of the Way'* to conquer in Damascus as many had fled to Damascus from Jerusalem. But as we shall see, things just didn't go the way Paul had envisioned, and his whole world and belief system changed radically not only for himself but also for those who knew him by reputation.

Paul was an ardent student of the Torah, a zealous Pharisee, but his encounter with Jesus Christ on that eventful day changed his life and theology forever. The most influential interpretation of Paul's conversion (transformation) is that it transformed not simply his view and understanding of Jesus Christ, the Son of God, but eventually his view and understanding of Jewish Law (the Torah).

He converted from a zealous practitioner of the Jewish Laws to a leading proponent who warned Gentile converts and Messianic Jews vehemently against the law.[24] We need only think of Paul's description of *what he had been: "exceedingly zealous for my ancestral traditions,"*[25] *"so far as righteousness (with) in the law was concerned, blameless,*[26] *and his turnaround in counting loss what had previously been counted as gain.*[27]

We recall also his assertion that (presumably during his

---

[23] Stanley, *Life Principles Bible*, Acts 9: 1,2.
[24] Ibid. Galatians 5: 1-12.
[25] Ibid. Galatians 1-14.
[26] Ibid. Philippians 3:6.
[27] Ibid. Philippians 3:7.

conversion), "I, through the Law died to the Law that I might live in God."[28] If a single text summed up his strong consensus position at this point, it would be found in Paul's Romans 10:4; *'Christ is the end of the law for righteousness to everyone who believes.'* *"The goal of the law was always to point us to the Savior,*[29] *which is why Jesus Christ is the fulfillment of the law. He is our righteousness; there is no holiness apart from Him. Jesus completely obeyed the law without exception and without fault, and His perfect, sinless record becomes ours through faith."*[30] What Paul concluded from his Damascus road encounter was 'Christ is the end of the (Jewish) law.'[31]

The importance of Paul's transformation is underscored by the fact that the Damascus road event is narrated three times in the book of Acts.[32] In all three accounts, Paul recalls on his approaching Damascus, *"He saw a light brighter than the sun, blazing around me and my companions. We all fell to the ground, and those who were with me saw the light but did not understand the voice of the One who was speaking to me.*

I heard a voice saying to me in Aramaic:

"Saul, Saul, why do you persecute Me: It is hard for you to kick against the goads (a Greek proverb for *useless resistance*)."

Paul asked, *"Who are you Lord?"*

Christ answered, **"I am Jesus the Nazarene, whom you are persecuting."**

And I said, *"What shall I do Lord?"*

---

[28] Stanley, *Life Principles Bible*, Galatians 2:9.
[29] Ibid. Romans 7:7.
[30] Ibid. LIFE LESSONS, Romans 10:4, p.1320.
[31] Dunn, *The Theology of Paul the Apostle,* p. 346.
[32] Stanley, *Life Principles Bible*, Acts 9:1-31, 22: 3-16, 26:12-18.

> Christ spoke, "**But get up and stand on your feet: for this purpose I have *appeared* to you to *appoint* you a minister and a witness not only to the things which you have seen, but also to the things in which I will *appear* to you; rescuing you from the Jewish people and Gentiles, to whom I am *sending* you, to open their eyes so that they may turn from the darkness to light, and from the dominion of Satan to God, that they may receive forgiveness of sins and an inheritance among those who have been sanctified by faith in Me.**"[33]

Paul was led into Damascus as his encounter with Jesus Christ left him blind. He was later visited by another devout observer of the law, *Ananias* who was highly respected by all Jews living in Damascus.

'Ananias stood beside me and said, "Brother Saul, receive your sight." And at that moment I was able to see.

> Then Ananias said, *"The God of our fathers has **appointed** you to know His will and to use the Righteous One and to hear words from His mouth. You will be His **witness** to all people of what you have **seen and heard**. Now, why do you delay? Get up, and be baptized and wash your sins away, calling on His name."*[34]

According to St. Luke in the Book of Acts, Paul started teaching and evangelizing in the synagogues in Damascus and Jerusalem. St. Luke wanted Paul to be *immediately* associated with the original apostles. *Paul denied this.*[35]

---

[33] Stanley, *Life Principles Bible*, Acts 26: 13-18.
[34] Ibid. Acts 22: 13-16.
[35] Ibid. Galatians 1:17.

Initially, Paul left Damascus and spent time in the deserts of the Sinai (Arabian Peninsula) as well as spending time in Damascus for a period of three years.[36] He needed a degree of solitude and time to collect his thoughts as to the commission of his future task as given him by Christ; he was not ready for what was to come. According to some historians, Paul may have started evangelizing in the desert area (modern day Jordan) known as the Nabatean Territory where he may not have been welcome with his new message and *'was asked to leave.'*

> *'Even during this three-year period, and later, wherever Paul traveled and spread his message, either a revival or rebellion ensued, and that was a pattern he laid claim to for the rest of his life.*[37]

---

[36] Ibid. Galatians 1: 15-18
[37] C. W. Briggs, *The Apostle Paul in Arabia*, (Balston Spa, New York, JSTOR, 1913), Vol. 41, No. 4 (April 1913), pp. 255-259.

The Way, Christianity A New Beginning

Paul affirmed his gospel came to him as a revelation from Jesus Christ.[38] Any analysis of Paul's thought that ignores this statement cannot do justice to his theology. Paul made it clear the specific revelatory event to which he referred was his encounter with Christ on the Damascus road and subsequently living in Arabia and Damascus for three years.[39]

He also indicated his dependence on other Christians for insights into his teachings. He clearly expressed his debt to believers in 2 Corinthians 1:11,12,[40] [41]and Philemon.[42] It is not likely Paul had contact with the 'earthly' Jesus, but it would be wrong however to use Paul's statement in 2 Corinthians 5:16,17 to suggest that he received *no* information from the earthly teachings of Jesus from those who *had* spent time with Jesus. Paul used this passage to state he no longer viewed Christ from *a 'fleshy, human' point of view*. Though he did not meet Jesus personally, he was clearly influenced by Jesus's teachings. The ethical teaching of Romans 12 has sections much like the Sermon on the Mount in the Book of Matthew.[43] The eschatological teachings in 1 Thessalonians 4-7 and 2 Thessalonians resemble Jesus's teachings in the Olivet Discourse of Mark 13 (also see Matthew 24, 25 and Luke 21). The Olivet Discourse is the name given to the orderly and extended teachings given by Jesus Christ on the Mount of Olives, and His subject concerned the *end of times*.[44] As Paul interprets, quotes, and

---

[38] Stanley, *Life Principles Bible,* Galatians 1: 11,12.
[39] Ibid. Galatians 1: 15-17.
[40] Ibid. 2 Corinthians 1: 11,12.
[41] Ibid. 1 Thessalonians 1: 1-4, 3:7.
[42] Ibid. Philemon 1:4-7.
[43] Ibid. Mathew 5, 6, 7.
[44] www.gotquestions.org/Olivet-discourse.htmp as of October 4, 2019.

alludes to the Old Testament and the prophets in his letters, he viewed it all regarding his revelation of God in Christ. The Greek world in which Paul was raised contributed and helped formulate the linguistic distinctives in his writings and philosophy (note the statement from Acts 17:28, 'for in Him we live and move and exist, as even some of your own poets have said, "For we also are His children."')

Paul's Jewish background also influenced his viewpoint and outlook. Neither Greek nor Hebrew thought, however, could provide the complete basis for Paul's teachings and theology. He clothed some of his statements in words taken from his Greek and Hebrew background, but his newfound faith in Christ caused him to view the entirety of his faith.[45]

Paul's belief system became *Christocentric* (centered in Christ). We can accurately summarize Paul's thoughts by using *"in Christ,"* a frequent phrase in Paul's letters. The foundation for Paul's theology was not ethics, anthropology, soteriology, ecclesiology, or eschatology. Underlying all these important themes was Paul's view that salvation was *"in Christ and the church is the body of Christ, only existing because believers are first in Christ."*[46]

Paul's thoughts can be described as historical, functional, and dynamic. His thoughts were historical because they were grounded in the historical events of the incarnation, life, death, and resurrection of Jesus.[47]

His theology is functional primarily because he emphasized functional aspects of Christ's work. Normally, Paul entered a description of Christ's *'being,'* or essence, only when he met a heretical challenge to his teachings. His description of Christ's person in Colossians 2:15-19 and 2:9,10 was a response to deprecation of Christ's personage. *'Paul warned the Colossians church to guard against empty, deceptive philosophies that were based on limited human reasoning. It may be impossible for us to comprehend*

---

[45] Lea and Black, *The New Testament*, pp.335-336.
[46] Stanley, *Life Principles Bible*, 1 Corinthians 12:26-28.
[47] Ibid. Galatians 4:4.

how Jesus could be totally human and totally divine at the same time (John 1:1,14; Philippians 2:6-8),' but that is the clear teaching of scripture, and we must accept it even if we do not understand it. Jesus said, "He who has seen Me has seen the Father." (John 14:9).'[48] Paul's theology also led to a dynamic, redemptive encounter with Christ. He did not emphasize theology for its own sake but to stress the urgency of a vital, living encounter with Christ (Colossians 3:1-5). 'Believers are admonished to focus our thoughts on the things that honor the Lord, because God's goal *is* to change us into the likeness of Christ, and that transformation begins in our minds.'[49]

We are now to the point of studying and presenting the various topics that comprise the theology of St. Paul; each topic builds one on another. We need to try to understand Paul's theology as it was written in his letters as they are the guides and *pathways* from which his theology can be derived.

The Book of Romans was considered Paul's 'grandest' work and, as many have said, 'it is his *Christian Manifesto*,' the Gospel of Jesus Christ. It was not directed at one church body, 'one in trouble or under attack by nonbelievers or Judaizers.' Some 'academics' and theologians imply Romans was written for his fellow Jews. Paul was disappointed his fellow Jews would not accept his new theology and accept Jesus Christ as the long- awaited Messiah.

The following headings will be discussed; some short and to the point while others may be more in depth and will require the reader to s-t-r-e-t-c-h their understanding and study:

- God and Mankind,
- Paul and his understanding of Adam,
- The law,
- The Gospel of Jesus Christ,
- Jesus and man,
- Christ crucified – the Risen Lord,
- The crucial transformation,

---

[48] Ibid. LIFE LESSONS, Colossians 2:9,10, P.1440.
[49] Stanley, *Life Principles Bible*, LIFE LESSONS, Colossians 3:2, p,1410.

- Justification by faith,
- Participation in Christ,
- Sanctification,
- Salvation,
- The Gift of the Spirit,
- Baptism,
- The Lord's Supper.

I will ask you '*not*' to get frustrated with the text and subject matter. The reader may find, as I have (and did), literally shaking my head, and asking, 'what have I just read; what am I to understand; can I make sense of this?' With thought, and a little patience, I promise it will!

Hopefully, one may find themselves questioning their own Christology, and I believe that is a good thing. I am confident you will come away from ***It's Not Rocket Science: The Theology of St. Paul the Apostle*** with a clearer understanding of St. Paul's Christian theology, and what Christ means in *your* life at a deeper level.

God and Mankind

A systematic study of Paul's theology *begins* with his belief in the one true God and Jesus Christ. That is not simply because the term *theology* may be said to have *'speech about God'* as its primary meaning. It is much more because God is the fundamental presupposition of Paul's theology, the starting point of his theologizing and a primary subtext of all his writing.[50]

As a rule in the Pauline letters, God is mentioned at once as the primary legitimating factor behind Paul's life work; *'Paul, called to be an apostle of Jesus Christ by the will of God;*[51] *'Paul, an apostle (not sent through an agency of man, but through Jesus Christ and God the Father, who raised Him from the dead), and all the brethren who are with me, to the churches of Galatia;*[52] and one that becomes almost stereotypical thereafter, *'Paul, an apostle of Christ Jesus by the will of God'.*[53] Whatever else Paul's theology was, *it was talk of Jesus Christ and God*. It isn't coincidental that the thematic statement in Romans is an affirmation of *'God's righteousness,'*[54] that one of the first main sections afterwards begins with 'God's wrath,'[55] and that the starting point of Paul's indictment is *'what may be known of God.*[56]

Paul did not need to explain his beliefs about God as they were already common to and shared with the disciples, believers, his readers, and followers. His speech about God was part of the shared speech of the first Christian congregations, already a

---

[50] Dunn, *The Theology of Paul the Apostle*, p.50.
[51] Stanley, *Life Principles Bible*, 1 Corinthians 1:1.
[52] Ibid. Galatians 1: 1,2.
[53] Ibid. Ephesians, 1:1.
[54] Ibid. Romans 1:17.
[55] Ibid. Romans 1:18-20.
[56] Ibid. Romans 1: 18,19.

fundamental 'taken-for- granted' of their common discourse.

One reason why Paul did not have to explain or defend his belief in God was it was the fundamental belief of his *own tradition*, a belief in which he had been instructed from youth and out of which he had lived his life for as long as he could remember. Paul's transition had not changed his belief in or about God; God was the *'creator God of Genesis who had also enlightened him (2 Corinthians 4:6, echoing Genesis 1: 1-3).'* The most fundamental Jewish belief is the oneness of God. Paul had been taught to recite the *Shema* from his youth as a daily confession*: 'Hear O Israel: The Lord is our God, or the Lord our God, the Lord is one!*'[57]

Paul's antipathy to idolatry is equally clear and expressed with characteristic Jewish fear, dismay, and scorn. Luke portrayed Paul in Athens as *'deeply distressed to see the city was full of idols and was quick to denounce idolatry.*[58] This picture was borne out of Paul's own recollection of how the Thessalonian believers had *'turned to God from idolatry.*[59]

The degree to which Paul's anthropology is interwoven into his theology can be illustrated from the *two most important terms* in Paul's anthropology – *body and flesh*. For the former extends across the whole of Paul's theology and can serve as an unexpected motif. Paul uses '*body*' to speak of the human body, ominously of 'the body of sin'[60] and the 'body of death,'[61] of Christ's body of flesh[62] and the resurrected body[63] of the sacramental bread;[64] and the body of the church as the body of Christ.[65]

As for '*flesh,*' the term is obviously crucial for Paul's understanding of how the gospel operates. Apart from anything

---

[57] Stanley, *Life Principles Bible*, Deuteronomy, 6:4.
[58] Ibid. Acts 17: 16, 29.
[59] Ibid. 1 Thessalonians 1: 9,10.
[60] Ibid. Romans 6:6.
[61] Ibid. Romans 7:23,24.
[62] Ibid. Colossians 1:22, 2:11.
[63] Ibid. 1 Corinthians 15:44.
[64] Ibid. 1 Corinthians 10:16,17.
[65] Dunn, *The Theology of Paul the Apostle*, p.52.

else, it clearly describes '*flesh as the force field*' opposed to the Spirit of God; to live '*according to the flesh*' is the antithesis of Christian living.[66] 'Jesus never intended us to live the Christian life by our own strength. Rather he gives us His life through His Spirit. God's grace does not change the nature of our sin; sin always leads to death. Instead, His grace enables us to rely on the power of His Spirit to put to death our sinful urges and desires.'[67]

The *flesh is soil* that produces corruption. '*For the one who sows to his own flesh will from the flesh reap corruption, but the one who sows to the Spirit will from the Spirit reap eternal life.*'[68] And yet, as we shall see, few terms have been more misunderstood and seldom has Paul's meanings been more misrepresented than in the translations of *sarx* (Greek), *flesh*.

Paul's anthropology is not a form of individualism; people are social beings, defined as persons by relationships. In Paul's perspective human beings *are as they are* by virtue of their relationship to God and the world. St Paul's gospel is of God in Christ, reconciling the world to Himself.

Another important principle in Paul's anthropology is the term *sōma* (Greek) or '*body*,' as used by Paul. In the twenty-first century the first meaning of the term *body* is usually interpreted as the individual material organism or corpse. Paul never used the term *sōma* to mean corpse. In Paul's own usage, *sōma*, like so many of his terms, has a spectrum of meaning. As we shall see, *soma* as denoting the human body included the physical body but is more than that.

'*A better term or word to use (to help break away from twenty-first century preconceptions) is the alternative term* **embodiment**, *soma as the embodiment of a person. In this sense, soma is a relational concept. It denotes the person embodied in a social environment and vice versa. It is the means of living-in or experiencing an environment;*

---

[66] Stanley, *Life Principles Bible*, Romans 8:4-13.
[67] Stanley, *Life Principles Bible,* LIFE LESSONS, Romans 8:13, p. 1317.
[68] Ibid. Galatians 6:8.

it means more than the physical body.'[69]

An analogy can be found in the application found in 1 Corinthians 15:42-44. The present body (the *embodiment* of the soul) ends in corruption, dishonor, weakness; the resurrected body (the *embodiment* of the Spirit)[70] is raised in incorruptibility, glory and power. The *soul* body takes after the *original Adam*, or earth, made of dust.

The *spiritual body* will be patterned after Christ's *resurrection body*.[71] Evidently the *soul* body, the present body (body of the flesh) as such cannot share in the kingdom of God; it is corruptible flesh and blood, and *'only the incorruptible, the spiritual body is capable of inheriting God's kingdom.'*[72]

Redemption for Paul was not some kind of escape from bodily existence but a *transformation* into a different kind of bodily existence - *the mystery of resurrection*.[73] *Body* is the common term, but not a fleshly body, a body made of dust, a corruptible or mortal body. This is only the embodiment, the embodiment appropriate to a physical world subject to decay and death.

The embodiment of the *resurrection body* will be different, i.e., an embodiment appropriate to the *world of Spirit*, beyond death. Or more sharply, life 'in the flesh' stands in contrast to being *'with Christ, which is far better.'*[74] *'Many in the Philippian culture feared death greatly, and just as many have a fear of death today. However, Paul was not afraid of death because he knew that "to be absent from the body means to be at home with the Lord' (2 Corinthians 5:8)."*

One area of contention concerning *'the flesh'* for Paul was the Jewish people's *'confidence in the flesh'* belonging to the people of Israel;[75] confidence in a national identity marked out by physical

---

[69] Dunn, *The Theology of St. Paul the Apostle*, p.56.
[70] Stanley, *Life Principles Bible*, Corinthians 15:45.
[71] Stanley, *Life Principles Bible*, 1 Corinthians 15: 45-49.
[72] Ibid. 1 Corinthians 15:50.
[73] Ibid. 1 Corinthians 15::51-54.
[74] Ibid. Philippians 1:22,23.
[75] Ibid. LIFE LESSONS, Philippians 1:23, p. 1396.

kinship by circumcision in the flesh.[76] As we shall see later, it is precisely the fact that circumcision *is in the flesh*, physical and visible,[77] denoting a religious identity conceived in such terms (Galatians 6:12,13) that explains Paul's later hostility to it.[78]

Two other words in Greek and Hebrew translation to Paul were *nous* (mind) and *kardia* (heart). Paul had a very literal and commanding understanding of Greek, and where there were sometimes *no* comparable words in Hebrew, he used Greek to formulate his ideas. The importance of the mind *(nous)* for Paul is easily documented. It is with his mind that he approved the laws of God.[79] The transformation of Christian existence comes through *'the renewal of the mind. Transformation begins with our thinking and with consciences that are committed to listening to and obeying God. Our minds are renewed as we study His Word, and our hearts are changed as we submit to Him. We do not merely try hard to sin less. We learn to depend upon Him, observe His commands, and trust Him to mold us into people who please Him. It is then we discover how awesome it is to live in the center of His will because it is life at its very best – and there is nothing in the human world that compares.*[80]

Worship should engage *the mind as well as the spirit.*[81] *The renewal of the mind* means not a new capacity to discern God's will by rational means but the integration of rationality within the total transformation of the person, the recovery of the mind's proper function from its *disqualified place.*

The term *kardia* (heart) is more characteristically Hebrew, but to a lesser degree Greek in both cases denoting the innermost part of the person, the *seat of emotions, but also of thought and will.* Paul's usage reflects this range of meaning. God is *'He who searches*

---

[76] Ibid. Philippians 3:3,4.
[77] Ibid. Romans 2:28.
[78] Dunn, *The Theology of St. Paul the Apostle*, p.68-69.
[79] Stanley, *Life Principles Bible*, Romans 7:23-25.
[80] Ibid. LIFE LESSONS, Romans 12:2, p. 1322, Ephesians 4:22,23.
[81] Ibid. 1 Corinthians 14:14,15.

the heart.'⁸² The law and circumcision must penetrate to the heart.

Likewise, obedience *and* belief need to be *from the heart*. 'If you confess with your mouth Jesus as Lord and believe in your heart that God raised Him from the dead, *you will be saved*. Salvation can only come through faith in Jesus Christ. You confess it with your mouth to put your faith into action and to affirm that you are accountable to Jesus Christ, who is now your Lord. You also believe in your heart that *He triumphed over death*. This means Christ *will save you*, has the authority to lead you and the wisdom to transform you.'⁸³

For Paul, the heart as the organ of decision making is evident in 1 Corinthians 7:37 and in 2 Corinthians 9:7. It was important for Paul that the experience of God's grace penetrate to the innermost depths of a person, and that the corresponding faith was an expression of deeply felt commitment.⁸⁴

In summation, Paul's conception of the human person is a being functioning within several dimensions. As embodied beings we are social, defined in part by our need and ability to have relationships, not as an option extra, but as a dimension of our very existence.

*'Our flesh-ness attests to our frailty and weakness as mere humans, the inescapable certainty of our death, our dependence on satisfaction of appetite and desire, or vulnerability to manipulation of the appetites and desires. At the same time as rational beings, we are capable of soaring to the highest heights of reflective thought. As experiencing beings, we are capable of the deepest emotions and the most sustained motivations. We are living beings, animated by the mystery of life as a gift, and there is a dimension of our being at which we are directly touched by the profoundest reality within and behind the universe – God.'*⁸⁵

Paul would no doubt say in thankful acknowledgment with the psalmist: *'I praise You, for I am fearfully and wonderfully made.'*⁸⁶

---

[82] *Ibid. Romans 8:27.*
[83] Stanley, *Life Principles Bible*, LIFE LESSONS, Romans 10: 9,10, p.1320.
[84] Dunn, *The Theology of Paul the Apostle*, pp. 74-75.
[85] Dunn, p. 78.
[86] Stanley, *Life Principles Bible*, Ps. 139:14.

The Law and The Term 'Adam' The Dark Side of Humanity

Paul showed awareness that Adam (*adam*) denoted humankind. The story of Adam and Eve in the Garden of Eden is the biblical story of the beginning of humankind. God gave Adam and Eve everything, including the *tree of life* and the *tree of knowledge*. As to scripture, Adam and Eve ate from the tree of knowledge, thus disobeying God's instructions '*not to*.' For this they were deprived of the opportunity to attain eternal life (Genesis 2:16,17). Humankind, in seeking to grasp God's glory (to be equal to God), had lost even the share in the glory it had originally been given.[87]

Between the time of Adam and the creation of the law, all was well with human society and no law needed to be applied; humankind enjoyed life,[88] and sin was disempowered, ineffective.[89] Summarily, Paul believed humankind in this world was not just weak but corruptible. This is the inescapable dimension if sin; failure and transgression (transgression is a term meaning to go beyond limits set or prescribed by divine law).

Humanity was created for a relationship with God, a relationship that is the essence of human life in relationship to God, and as humans in relation to the rest of the world. Paul used Adam to illustrate that humankind had made the mistake of thinking it could achieve a more satisfying relationship with the world if it freed itself from its relationship with God. This is the trap and an idea many who deem themselves intellectual fall into in our day and time. Paul's indictment of humankind starts in the first section of Romans – Romans 1:18-3:20. The human condition Paul had

---

[87] Dunn, *The Theology of St. Paul the Apostle*, 94.
[88] Stanley, *Life Principles Bible*, Genesis 2:7.
[89] Dunn, p. 94.

in mind was marked *not only by weakness but also by ungodliness*, the term he used in the indictment (Romans 1:18: *'For the wrath of God is revealed from heaven against all ungodliness of men who suppress the truth in unrighteousness'*).[90]

Humans beings were literally *'without worship, lacking in reverence.'* They were marked by unrighteousness and absence of goodness, the former term echoing the opening indictment of Romans 1:18. There was something fundamentally unjust in their relationships. Worst of all, in a clearly intended climax to the sequence, human beings were *'sinners'* and *'enemies of the Spirit of God.'*[91]

Again, in Ephesians 2:1-3, Paul uses powerful imagery to characterize humankind:

> *'You were dead in your trespasses and sins, in which you once walked in accordance with this world, in accordance with the prince of the power of the air, the spirit which is now at work in the sons of disobedience; among them we too all formerly lived in the flesh and of the mind, and were by nature children of wrath, even as we rest.'*[92]

Rabbis, including Paul described the actions of humans as an *'evil impulse within'* to explain the mad, self-damaging choices we all make. Paul's attempt to explain this 'dark side of humanity' focuses on the figure of *Adam* and the account of *'man's first disobedience'* in Genesis 3; what has been traditionally described as *'the fall from Grace,'*[93] trying to have a satisfying relationship with the world if it freed itself from its relationship with God. This is the trap and idea that many who deem themselves intellectual fall into today.

---

[90] Stanley, *Life Principles Bible*, Romans 1:18.
[91] Dunn, *The Theology of St. Paul the Apostle*, pp. 80-81.
[92] Stanley, *Life Principles Bible*, Ephesians 2:1-3.
[93] Ibid. Genesis 3.

'Too many people reject the truth because it interferes with their lifestyle. They participate in every form of sin attempting to satisfy their needs, but all they are doing is moving farther away trying fill an empty void within themselves – what only the Lord can do. Even deeper emptiness, dissatisfaction, and hopelessness always result. Eventually those transgressions take over their lives and destroy them.' [94]

Man turned from God and focused exclusively on the world revolting against its role as a creature *derived from grace* and thinking he could stand as creator in his own right. In consequence humankind had fallen when thought to rise, had become foolish, not wise, baser, and not superior. It had denied its likeness to God and preferred the likeness of beasts.

'It had lost its share in the majesty of divinity and now falls far short of what it might have become. Instead of sharing eternal life, it had become dominated by death, a sucker for sin. It shares in a pervasive out-of-joint-ness, frustration, and futility with the rest of creation. Such was Paul's indictment of humankind as he first laid out in Romans 1:18-29.' [95]

The first chapter of Romans lays out the indictment for mankind, and it starts with Paul's idea that a primary law was being breached by Adam and all mankind. Paul believed that '***desire conceives** (to covet)*' and gives birth to sin. This thought provides an explanation for why Paul often focused on the tenth commandment of the Decalogue: *'You shall not covet…'* (Exodus 20:17; Deut. 5:21).[96] In other words, Paul shared the wider belief that the primal sin was wrong desire; that's what the serpent appealed to in the Garden; Adam's coveting of divine status: *'You shall be like God.'* [97]

From Romans 2:1-29 and Romans 3:20, Paul basically claims that all people are condemned, not just the immoral but the moral as well as the Jewish people. Keeping the law is not the answer

---

[94] Stanley, *Life Principles Bible*, LIFE LESSONS, Romans 1:24, p.1307.
[95] Dunn, Romans 1:18-32, p.99.
[96] Stanley, *Life Principles Bible*, Exodus 20:17, Deuteronomy 5:12.
[97] Ibid. Genesis 3:5.

to salvation, and neither is it enough to allow a sinner to escape judgment. People's secret sins will be judged by the gospel and God.

When God judges, it is always according to the truth, in full accordance with the facts. Moralist may try to hide the facts, but God always exposes them. Since the judgment of God is according to the truth, it is foolhardy for moralists to believe that God will judge others and not them. To put oneself in the position of the moralist would mean to despise God's kindness, forbearance, and patience. The goodness of God leads us to repentance.

In judging others, moralist have completely missed the purpose of God's goodness. They are unaware of their own needs for repentance. Throughout scripture, God tells us that He will save the humble but oppose the proud (2 Samuel 22:26-28; Proverbs 3:34; James 4:6; 1 Peter 5:5).[98] The proud try to assume God's place, *and that He will never allow!*

God will reward us according to our deeds.[99] Paul's comment about perseverance in doing good has some to question Paul's commitment to salvation by faith alone. But we need not worry. Perseverance in doing good does not mean that we are saved by doing good. Paul is expressing an eternal truth - *obedience to God does well in every dispensation.*[100]

The eternal truth is that God deals in condemnation without favoritism. Respect of a person simply means *partiality*. God is impartial in that He does not change His pattern 'to show the Jew first,' whether righteousness or unrighteousness is involved.

Here's how the principle of divine impartiality is applied: *for all those who have sinned without the Law will also perish without the Law; and all who have sinned under the Law will be judged by the Law.*[101] Unchecked and unatoned, sin leads to perdition (eternal

---

[98] Stanley, *Life Principles Bible*, 2 Samuel 22:26-28, Proverbs 3:34, James 4:6, 1 Peter 5:5.
[99] Ibid. 2 Corinthians 5:10.
[100] 'Dispensation' – the divine ordering of the affairs of the world; an appointment, arrangement, or favor, as by God.
[101] Stanley, *Life Principles Bible*, Romans 2:12.

damnation) whether we are Jewish and living under the law or are Gentile and living apart from the law.

Being moral is insufficient to being righteous. These *are not* synonymous concepts. Moral people may possess a heightened conscience and *live in the light of it*, but God demands righteousness, not just morality. Since no one innately possesses such righteousness, God deals with the moral and the immoral in the same way. Both fall short of God's glory.[102] 'While moralists may be better citizens, they are not better candidates for heaven. The human need for righteousness permeates both blatant sinners and moralists.'[103]

---

[102] Ibid. LIFE LESSONS, Romans 3:23, p.1310.
[103] Woodrow Kroll, *The Book of Roman-Righteousness in Christ* (Chattanooga, TN: AMG Publishers, 2002), Chapter 5.

Sin and The Law

In the absence of law, is there sin? Sin's definition in the Oxford English Dictionary is *'an immoral act considered to be a transgression against divine law, or the Law of God.*'[104] Again, a transgression (to transgress) is *'to go beyond the limits set by a moral principle, standard, or law.*'[105]

Between the time of Adam (all mankind) and the law given to Moses, there was no written law. Was mankind before the existence of laws given to Moses and the Torah, exempt from the law? Paul may have said, *'absolutely not,'* as there is still the *law of God*.

> *'The Law of Moses was powerless to actually deliver anyone from the powers of sin that had its roots in the flesh, since all it could do was "define" what was good. Paul put his own "life in the Spirit of Christ" forward as a model for his followers to imitate and was often disappointed in their seeming inability to "walk in the spirit," since they failed to exhibit even the minimum standards of righteous behavior.*'[106]

I believe all humankind, whether-or not, they have been exposed to *'the law,'* innately inherit, or know the difference between right and wrong; even those we observe to be of primitive cultures. Human beings are made in the image of God – God is good, loving, perfect.

St. Paul's indictment of humanity tells us humankind is

---

[104] *Concise Oxford English Dictionary,* 12th Edition (Oxford University Press, 2011).
[105] Ibid. *transgression.*
[106] James D. Tabor, *Paul and Jesus* (New York: Simon and Schuster, 2012), p.17.

susceptible to God's wrath. Humans who do not abide by the *'innate principles'* of God's laws and disobey God's laws and are disobedient to God will suffer the consequences of God's wrath.

In focusing on the term *'sin,'* two remarkable features should be noted in the book of Romans:

- The first is the predominance of the term *'sin'* in the book of Romans,
- The second feature worthy of preliminary note is the 'striking personification of sin' in Romans is almost equally as unusual in other of Paul's epistles written later (Ephesians, Philippians, Colossians, Philemon, and the *'Pastoral letters'* to Timothy and Titus), where the plural usage (sins) predominates.[107]

Paul had, and expressed a tremendous sense of sin as a power that bore down upon him as well as humankind. In particular, sin is the power that makes human beings forget their *creatureliness* and *dependence* on God; the power that preventing humankind from recognizing its true nature and deceived Adam into thinking he was godlike and made him unable to grasp that he was but *adamah* (ground, earth).

Sin is the power that turns humankind upon itself with a preoccupation of satisfying and compensating for its own weakness as flesh. It is that power that has caused countless individuals of goodwill, but inadequate resolve to cry out in despair: *"I can't help it! I can't fight it!"*[108] Sin simply *'entered the world…' (Romans 5:12)*[109]; it came to life. *'I was one alive apart from the Law; but when the commandment came, sin became alive and I died.'*[110] That is all Paul believed he needed to say.

We should not think Paul envisioned the power of sin only in

---

[107] Dunn, *The Theology of St. Paul the Apostle*, p.111.
[108] Ibid. pp. 112-113.
[109] Stanley, *Life Principles Bible*, Romans 5:12.
[110] Ibid. Romans 7:9.

individualistic terms. The indictment of Romans 1:18-32 is all about relationships. Neither did Paul think in terms of modern era ideas of institutional sins; the power of sin (injustice and manipulation) possibly entrenched in social institutions. He believed he lived in a world as an organized system of social values that did not recognize God, very much like the world we live in today.

"Paul believed that humankind lived out its life in the service of sin, whose payoff is death" (Romans 6:23).[111] Our sin has earned us death. Either you pay it or forfeit your life, or Jesus pays it and gives eternal life (Matthew16:25, 26). *You make the choice. All our good works cannot earn us a place in heaven.* Our only hope is to *'receive the gift that Jesus Christ has purchased for us on the Cross'* (John 3:16-18).[112]

Paul also believed that sin *is a partner of the law*. The law defined what is considered sin; therefore, the law, sin, and death are all interrelated. When Paul talks of death, he's referring to the physical body, or flesh that has died. There is nothing to look forward to – the end - a total absence of the love of God.

Trying to understand Paul's theology concerning the law is a central theme in Romans. When he uses the triumvirate of law, sin, and death when writing or speaking initially in Romans and other epistles, he is driving his formulaic genius concerning the aspects of sin.

Paul, in Romans and other epistles, describes what constitutes sin(s). As mentioned in the discussion of Adam, coveting and what it may lead one to, and idolatry are Paul's primary consideration of sin. Misdirected religions and religious beliefs, or the refusal to worship the one true God, he believed was a perversion of a creature's basic instinct not to acknowledge God and not to acknowledge dependence on God.

The link between idolatry and sexual license was well established in Jewish folklore and carried over into Christianity.

---

[111] Dunn, *The theology of St. Paul the Apostle*, p.129.
[112] Stanley, *Life Principles Bible*, LIFE LESSONS, 6:23, p. 1314.

Independence from God can quickly become commitment to self-indulgences or rather slavery to self-indulgences.

Paul believed the most characteristic expression of self-indulgence and desire is sexual activity. This is the clear implication of Romans 1:24: 'God handed them over in the desires of their hearts to the uncleanliness of dishonoring their bodies among themselves.'[113] Uncleanliness and impurity typically denoted sexual immorality, and the 'dishonoring the bodies among themselves' likewise presumably refers to sexual activities in which people treat themselves (their bodies) with lack of respect.[114] Passion and lust lead to sexual immorality.

Paul believed passionately about a form of sexual irregularity – homosexual practice among both men and women– *the fruit of disgraceful passions*. To this point early Jewish and early Christian tradition stood out against the Greco-Roman culture, where homosexual practice was quite acceptable and even highly regarded, seemingly much as we see it portrayed today by individuals and organizations who condone the practices.

In contrast, the Jewish reaction - *it is a perversion,* a pagan abomination is consistent. To be noted is the fact that Paul speaks only of homosexual acts. He says nothing about homosexual orientation itself, only about the indulgence of 'desires (Romans 1:24), passions (Romans 1:26), and sexual desire.' In 1 Corinthians 6:9 three terms are used to list unacceptable lifestyles – "adulterer, effeminate (men) and practicing homosexuals."[115] [116]

A question may be pondered as to the following: God is Good, God is perfect, and humankind was made in the image of God.

Where *do* homosexuals fit into the equation; what are they to believe? Outside of marriage between a man and women, Paul proposed *celibacy*.

Left to itself, free of God, the human mind is incapable to

---

[113] Stanley, *Life Principles Bible,* Romans 1:24.
[114] Dunn, *The Theology of St. Paul the Apostle,* p.121.
[115] Dunn, p. 122.
[116] Stanley, *Life Principles Bible,* 1 Corinthians 6:9.

exercise the discernment and discrimination on which decision making depends. The results are inappropriate and unfitting judgments. Paul illustrates the effect of this in a *vice list* found in Romans 1:29-31.[117] The list contains twenty-one vices *from 'unrighteousness and greed -to faithless, loveless and merciless.'* Such *vice lists* were common in Judaism including those found in 1 Corinthians 5:10,11,1 Corinthians 6:9,10 and Galatians 5:19-21. The diversity of the items in these lists indicated that Paul did not have a *standard catalog* each time but varied them at least on occasion to speak more directly to concerns in the churches and communities written to.[118]

Paul hints *while laying it on the line*, describing sin and the abomination of some in mankind, that there is another way, and this *new message and gospel* was his commission directly from Jesus Christ *to all people in the world*, both Jews and Gentiles. In the New Testament, God's plan of salvation is called *'the way of the Lord.'*

The Way was the name given to the movement to which believers and followers of Jesus Christ subscribed after His death and resurrection. In Acts 11:26, the followers of *the Way* were first called *Christians* at the church in Antioch, Syria in AD 43-44 while Paul and Barnabas were ministering in that church body.[119] Paul's Damascus road experience occurred approximately eleven years earlier.

---

[117] Ibid. Romans 1:29-31.
[118] Dunn, *The Theology of St. Paul the Apostle*, p.124.
[119] Stanley, *Life Principles Bible*, Acts 11:26.

A New Gospel, "*The Way*," and A Way to Holiness

'Paul's indictment of *'humankind'* had been fierce. All humanity lives its life on earth under the power of sin. All humanity finds itself drawn inexorably whether by some primeval instinctive disposition or by its own will to self- destruction into a sagacity (*acute awareness*) of gratifying the flesh, what it knew to be right, and disowning God. All humanity, Jew as well as Gentile, stands under the condemnation of God's law and consequently is liable to God's judgment.

As a statement of charges against humankind, that was a bleak prospectus. Paul spends as much time as he does in drawing it up in Romans 1:18–3:20, not simply because his view of mankind *was* pessimistic. To such an accusation, Paul may have replied, "to the contrary;" he was simply being realistic, and the failure to recognize this reality is a fatal flaw in all idealistic or utopian visions.

And reviewing the history of "man's inhumanity to man" and abuse of creation, who could blame him? But the main reason Paul could be so devastatingly critical of humankind was no doubt his conviction that he knew the appropriate response to that indictment; not a defense, but *a response of grace* that fully dealt with the charges. "Just as sin ruled in death, so also, grace will reign through righteousness to eternal life (Romans 5:21)."[120]

The purpose of Paul's apostleship was "to bring about the obedience of faith among all Gentiles for His name's sake."[121] Paul wanted to bring the Gentile nations (*and his fellow Jews*) of the world into obedience to the faith (i.e., the body of the doctrine he was *appointed* to deliver).

---

[120] Dunn, *The Theology of St. Paul the Apostle*, p. 164.
[121] Stanley, *Life Principles Bible*, Romans 1:5.

Paul did regard his apostolic calling as a heavenly gift. It was the *grace given to him by God*. He did not seek the calling, he did not pray for it, but once it was *appointed* to him, he used his intellect, past learning, God's inspiration, and physical strength to spread the Gospel of Jesus Christ.

The righteousness of God is imparted because of faith in God and Jesus Christ; justification is a gift through the grace of God. Paul gets to his message in his letter to the Roman church, "The only way one can be justified before God is by faith through Christ (in Christ)." God will justify everyone who trusts in Him by faith apart from works.

No one can boast of salvation by human works or by keeping 'the law.' Paul's description in Romans presents the gospel of God "which He promised beforehand through His prophets in the holy scriptures."[122] The gospel was not an innovation of the Messianic Jews or new believers and followers of *the Way* (Christians). It had been preannounced by the Old Testament prophets from Genesis 3:15 to Malachi 4:2.

By quoting sixty-one times from the Old Testament, Paul told the Jews their scriptures were speaking of Jesus Christ just as much as the followers of the Nazarenes were. The gospel concerns God's Son, Jesus Christ.[123] The gospel is not about Jesus Christ; *the gospel is Jesus Christ*.

In Romans 1, Paul mentions Christ was born and 'declared' the Son of God with power. The word *declared* (Greek, *horizo*) has the meaning of 'appointed, or marked out by unmistakable signs.' It was used in Acts 10:42 and 17:31 as to Christ's appointment as judge.

There was a time when Jesus Christ was not yet born of the family of David, but there was never a time when He was not the Son of God. Christ was not born, but *eternally is* God the Son from the beginning of time to the end of times. The fact that Jesus

---

[122] Stanley, *Life Principles Bible*, Romans 1:2.
[123] Ibid. Romans 1:3,4.

is God the Son graphically and unmistakably was revealed to the world "by the resurrection from the dead, according to the Spirit of Holiness."[124]

---

[124] Ibid. Romans 1: 2-5.

FINALLY, You're a Christian 'Walking the Walk' - Pathways

We've come to the 'final chapters' of *It's Not Rocket Science: The Theology of St. Paul the Apostle.* My hope is you have a good grasp of who St. Paul the man was, his views on mankind, and why he spent much of his life tirelessly and fearlessly spreading the gospel of Jesus Christ to the world. If you're a Christian or are contemplating accepting Jesus Christ as your savior and accept the premise of 'walking the walk' with Christ, you will enjoy the remainder of the book. Your life and world *will* change. You may not have an encounter to the likes of St. Paul's on the Damascus road, but your *life, soul and heart* will be transformed in magnificent fashion forever – I promise!

God loves you and all His creation. 'He wants to make your life a blessing and wants you to have *faith and accept* Jesus Christ as your 'Lord and Savior.' At this point, if a new Christian, the Spirit of the Lord *will* move into your **heart, mind and soul.** You made a choice, so 'get up and stand on your feet.'[125]

So, what's next? What are you to do; how are you to build your relationship with God and Jesus Christ? These were questions that I needed answered many years ago, and unfortunately, I did not understand the gift concepts of 'God's free grace and of eternal life' given me, or why, I did not ask the right questions, or those who were to guide me in my 'walk with Christ' lacked the know-how of what I needed to know, or how to guide me personally. Fortunately, I found *'it is never too late,'* and I continue, as you will, to grow in faith, sanctification, and 'walking–the walk' with God and Jesus Christ…… with a bit of advice.

---

[125] Stanley, *Life Principles Bible*, Acts 26:16.

I was baptized when ten years old as were many of my fellow Sunday school friends. I cannot speak for the others, but the advice given to me, and possibly to others was, 'Now, you have to be a good little boy (or girl), and God will love you. If not, God will punish you!' I can only speak for myself.

Attending church was a weekly affair in my family *until* I 'hit the rebellious teen years.' For whatever reasons at the time, I found other things I felt were more important, and my attendance record was dismal. Unfortunately, my relationship with my God and Jesus Christ didn't get much better even into my adult years, and it very well could have been disastrous for my spiritual life.

Many Christians fall into the same traps and unfortunately forgot, or never really understood the awesome gift given them by Jesus Christ upon accepting Him as their Lord and Savior, baptized in His name. We attend church, meet and socialize with others in this 'body of Christ,' observe their mannerisms and speech, thinking 'this is what it's all about.' No wonder many tend to stray or simply walk out. Many Christians who attend a church don't even know the name of their pastor, or if asked, 'where is your church located?' – they can't give directions – or don't know!

One of the primary goals of **It's Not Rocket Science** is **not** to let you 'fall by the wayside or walk away.' My hope is the following information will give you guidance and instruction with your walk with Jesus Christ and God built on scripture, study (especially the Bible), and lead you on pathways to righteousness, sanctification and salvation. Most of the information given in the remaining paragraphs of this chapter came from sermons, sermon notes, and writings from Dr. Charles Stanley and his website **Intouch.org**.[126]

Who is God? Who is Jesus Christ? What is the Holy Spirit? These are all things you need to know. And, as a Christian, or soon to be baptized, you should seriously contemplate the following (*all Pathways*):

---

[126] Dr. Charles Stanley, *I Am Saved – Now What?* In Touch Ministries, (Atlanta, Georgia), January 9, 2015.

- <u>Read and study your Bible - Daily</u>! This is the source of information and inspiration to feed your spiritual needs,

- <u>Pray</u> for your needs and those you love. *Tell God you love Him.* Ask God to provide you with the leadership you need to help you walk with Jesus Christ – 'to live in the likeness of Christ.' God answers all prayers; the 'little ones' you may believe are too small for Him to care about, and the 'big ones;' God wants to hear from you, and *'God will answer your prayers.'* Prayers may be answered quickly; others, you will have to learn patience. If your prayer concerns what *'God's plan'* is for your life, He will inspire you, work with you, and give you all the power you need to complete the task,

Come with a focus on the Heavenly Father. When you praise the Lord, your mind lets go of earthly concerns and centers on His desires and glory.

Surrender To Him As Lord and King. The goal of prayer is not to get God to do what you want but to align your desires and requests with His will. Such prayers are the ones He promises to answer.

Approach the Lord With A Humble Dependent Spirit. Recognize that He is the one who provides for your needs and sustains your life.

Seek His Forgiveness And Protection From Temptation. Ask God to uncover anything unholy in your life and replace it with righteousness.

Developing a consistent prayer life takes commitment. Daily activities will crowd out time with the Lord unless you reserve a segment of each day to pray. (In Touch Daily Readings for Devoted Living, March 2021 "The Priority of Prayer," Luke 11:1-4)

- <u>If you need to be baptized</u>, **get baptized**.[127] Christ appeared to the eleven remaining disciples *after* His resurrection and 'commissioned' them to "go throughout the world and teach the gospel, and he who believes and *is baptized* will be saved.,"[128] (you may quote Jesus Christ and scripture on this)

- <u>Join a church</u> – one that teaches the 'word of God, has praise for the Holy Spirit – a Bible based church.' By attending church, frequently, you will be filling and nourishing your mind *with* the Holy Spirit, and grow in your spiritual life - finding a sense of peace and joy,

- <u>Tithing</u> We can never 'out give' what God has given us. Give when you can and as much as you can. You will find that what you give will be returned in ways unexpected. We owe God *this responsibility*. St. Paul was very conscience of collecting money and gifts for the very poor in Jerusalem throughout his missions; he was setting the example.[129] The Bible references giving 10% in Genesis 28: 20-22, "I will give a tenth to you."

- <u>Tell others what Jesus Christ means to you</u>. Initially, this may be tough to do (I'll admit that). Somewhere in your past, you decided to give your life *and obedience* to Jesus Christ – Why? Start there. There are books that may guide

---

[127] Stanley, *Life Principles Bible,* Matthew 3:13-17, Matthew 28: 18,19, Mark 16:16, Acts 10:38, Romans 6:4, Ephesians 4:4-6.
[128] Ibid. Mark 16: 15,16.
[129] Brittle, *The Right Man at the Right Time 3rd Edition,* 'St. Paul and the Collection,' p. 84.

you[130], and churches like the one I attend, First Baptist Clermont (Clermont, FL) offering classes helping believers to 'learn' how to witness – my hope is your church will do the same.

In time, if you're seriously living a life 'centered in Jesus Christ,' those around you will notice: your family, your friends, your coworkers.

Who is <u>God</u>?

Trying to define the essence of God could keep your mind occupied for hours, days, weeks, years. Everyone, believers and non-believers, who 'thinks' they have the answer, I'd love to hear your 'opinion.' In the movies, our Native American brothers and sisters often refer to the 'Great Spirit' that provided needs and offered wisdom. That's a good start. They relied on nature, the sun, moon, and stars to answer the questions important to their civilization. They looked up to see the day and night cosmos wondering 'what's out there defining their lives?'

We do the same today in a sense, but with today's science and technology when looking out into the universe, we *try to* see, and may wonder how incomprehensibly huge the universe is. Our country has sent 'space probes' out into just our solar system; some launched in decades past travelling at incredible speeds, and these probes are just reaching the outer planets. Who, *or what* created all this? Why? And how is mankind supposed to fit in. Most of what follows is taking and looking at the answer from a theological point of view.

---

[130] D. James Kennedy, *Evangelism Explosion* Fourth Edition (Tyndale House Publishers, Inc. Carol Stream, Illinois), 1996.

In scripture, God is referred to as the *'Trinity'* – **God the Father, God the Son,** and **God the Holy Spirit**. Each has its own meaning but are tied together as a whole.

- **'God the Father'** is the creator; He is the sovereign ruler of the universe and all encompassed within – everything. He is *'**omnipotent**** (God is infinite power and energy in the universe),[131] ***omnipresent*** (His presence is everywhere),[132] and ***omniscient*** (all knowing; He knows past, present, and future).[133] God is always with you, and at no point are you helpless or alone – *never!*

    If God tells you to do something, God assumes responsibility for providing you the means to make *His will* come true. Pray, Listen, Trust and Obey.

- **'God the Son'** is our Savior and Lord Jesus Christ. The person and place of Jesus Christ in our lives is the 'incarnate Son of God' (Jesus came to earth 'embodied in flesh or given a bodily, especially a human form'). Jesus walked among mankind; He humbled Himself as a man and a servant and 'became obedient to the point of death, even the death of the cross.'[134] And, Jesus was *sinless*. 'Therefore, God has highly exalted Him and given Him the name which is above every name, that at the name of Jesus every knee should bow, of those in heaven, and those on earth, and of those under the earth; and that every tongue should confess that Jesus Christ is Lord, to the glory of God the Father.'[135]

    If you're not a member of the clergy in 'a body of Christ

---

[131] Stanley, *Life Principles Bible*, Jeremiah 32: 17,27.
[132] Ibid. Psalms 139: 7-12.
[133] Ibid. 1 John 3:20.
[134] Ibid. Philippians 2: 8.
[135] Ibid. Philippians 2: 9-11.

– the church,' you're considered a *'layman,'* and assume a position of *'follow-ship.'* When Jesus came upon Peter and his brother Andrew tending their nets while fishing, 'He said to them, Follow Me, and I will make you fishers of men.'[136] When you accept the Lord Jesus Christ as your Savior, you are to *follow* Him in your walk and life, to work *towards* your ongoing sanctification. You are to live your life, Christ-like.

When you assume this position of *follow-ship*, you're making 'Jesus number one,' and He's your Boss. He has the authority to call all the 'plays in your life, and the right to tell you where to go.' As your boss, He has the authority, power, and *enablement* to tell you what to do, and with His power He will enable you to do whatever task for the Glory of God. Some may say, 'There's a lot of responsibility by becoming a Christian and following Jesus Christ; is it worth it?' – you better believe it!

By our very nature, we came to earth as sinners. If we came to earth as sinners, what did it cost God to fix the problem of our sins. It cost the 'death of His Son on the cross,' and with that, God and Jesus Christ 'paid for our sins in full.' In return, do we have responsibilities to God the Father and Jesus Christ? You better believe it!

- **God, the Holy Spirit** is the entity that took residence in your heart and soul upon your acceptance of Jesus Christ as your Savior. 'Christ has been given to us as an everlasting promise, and God will never leave nor forsake us, no matter what happens.[137] [138] [139]

---

[136] Stanley, *Life Principles Bible,* Matthew 4:18,19.
[137] Ibid. 'What the Bible Says About HOW THE HOLY SPIRIT GUIDES US,' p 1282.
[138] I bid. John 14:16-18, 1 Corinthians 3:16; 6:17; 2 Corinthians 1:21, 22; 5:5,
[139] Ephesians 1:13; 4:30, 1 John 4:2, 13. 139 Stanley, *Life Principles Bible*, Romans 8:26-29.

Though God's Word may not make sense to you, He will show you what they mean.[140] If there is something in you that is hardening God's work, He will reveal it to you.[141] When you feel inadequate, He bestows you with the giftedness you need to live the Christian Life.[142] And distress - the Holy Spirit can energize, encourage, and empower you to overcome whatever afflicts you.'[143] Therefore, don't hinder the Holy Spirit – He is your Helper, and His guidance is yours for the asking - through prayer. Whenever you need Him, pray, listen, follow His directions, and you can be sure that He will *never* lead you astray.

---

[140] Ibid. 1 Corinthians 2:12-14.
[141] Ibid. John 16:8.
[142] Ibid. 1 Corinthians 12: 4-11.
[143] Ibid. Romans 5:3-5

Baptism

James Dunn starts with a traditional view of baptism. 'In our analysis of Paul's understanding of the crucial transition, the beginning of salvation, there has been one notable omission. We have observed Paul's regular recall of his followers to the decisive event from which they dated their lives as Christians. We have examined the three main aspects that make up Paul's integrated view of this beginning and its consequences – justification by faith, participation in Christ, and the gift of the Spirit. But, the traditional label for this beginning has been "*baptism.*"

Most studies in this area assume that Paul would have thought of it in the same way. More determinative is the assumption that any reference back to conversion and initiation was bound to be the reference back to the event of baptism. Paul used allusions to baptism with metaphors like washing, anointing, sealing, and putting on clothes. These were all images of baptism.[144]

Baptism is a *sacrament*. In all historic Christian traditions, a sacrament is understood *as a subtle interrelation of spiritual and material*. The sacrament is *not* simply the ritual act.

The sacrament, properly speaking, is the inner as well as the outward act. Baptism denotes the spiritual reality symbolized by the ritual, and not merely symbolized, but in some sense brought to actuality in the event. *That is what baptism means.* That is why baptism is the most obvious single term to describe the whole. And since the sacrament, by definition, embraces the whole, it is natural to refer metaphors of becoming Christian to it and natural to refer to the blessings related to baptism.

One of the early issues surrounding the ritual of baptism was many believed that to be baptized, they were embraced in all that was

---

[144] Dunn, *The Theology of Paul the Apostle*, pp. 442-443.

involved in the crucial transition to salvation (justification, union with Christ, the gift of the Spirit) through the single act of baptism. It is being squeezed 'concertina-like' until all that is really in view is the ritual act itself – baptism in its original sense of immersion.

It is interesting that Paul deemphasized baptism. It was Paul himself who resisted any possible analogy between Christian baptism and equivalent cultic rites in the mysteries. Baptism provided no such bond, only with the name of Jesus. Baptism provided no such guarantee. Paul even expresses his gratitude that he baptized so few. He could recall baptizing only Lydia in Philippi, Crispus and Gaius,[145] and he mentions the household of the Philippian jailer and his family in Philippi.[146]

So far as Paul was concerned, his mission was to preach the gospel, not to baptize – an interesting comment on the role and relative importance attributed by Paul to baptism within the complex of conversion and initiation. Baptism is/was the first step of living a life "in Christ." Living a life in Christ of those baptized is the *beginning* of their journey through justification, sanctification – to salvation and holiness.

On any analysis of the traditional history lying behind this talk of being baptized in the Spirit, there is one obvious trail to be followed though surprisingly neglected by most commentators. It is the trail that begins in the tradition of John the Baptist's most striking utterance: *"As for me, I baptize you with water; but He (the Coming One) who is mightier than I, and I am not fit to untie the thong of His sandals; He will baptize you with the Holy Spirit and Fire."*[147] This predication is recalled in all four gospels, the only feature of the Baptist's preaching for which this is true. We may deduce that it was a saying particularly cherished within the communities who transmitted the tradition.[148]

The imagery of being baptized in Spirit is both coined as a metaphor from the rite of baptism and set in some distinction

---

[145] Stanley, *Life Principles Bible*, 1 Corinthians 1:14.
[146] Ibid. Acts 16:27-33.
[147] Ibid. Luke 3:16.
[148] Dunn, *The Theology of Paul the Apostle*, p. 451.

from, or even antithesis to, the rite of baptism. The consistent form of the gospel saying contrasts John's baptizing *in water* with the Coming One's baptizing *in Spirit*.

In the metaphorical adaptation, Spirit takes the place of water, the *'in'* in which the individual is immersed. The reception of the Spirit was generally a vivid experience in the remembered beginnings of Christian commitment, and Paul refers to it repeatedly and could do so precisely because it was such a striking highlight in his transition. To receive the 'gift of the Spirit' was to be 'stamped' with the seal of new ownership, a stamp whose effects made visible who it was to whom the individual now belonged.

One of the more difficult aspects of Paul's theology is the fact that it seems to have little if any room for infant baptism. From one perspective this was almost inevitable, for Paul was a missionary and church founder. Baptism in his experience was an *evangelistic* rather than a *pastoral* act. Typically for him baptism was the initiation of newly believing followers, mainly adults, into church bodies newly formed.[149] Today, there are denominations that perform the rite and sacrament of infant baptism, and I believe (and there are those who disagree) it is the right of the denomination in question, and I find the ceremony quite beautiful with proud parents and relatives attending. I also believe, as did Paul, baptism is the initial beginning of *one's life living in Christ.* My hope is the parents and caregivers of the infant are *in Christ* and rear the child *totally in Christ.*

At this point if you're contemplating baptism and have made the decision and commitment to follow Jesus Christ for the rest of your life, both mortal and eternal, **get baptized.** The following four chapters are *'what's in it for you.'* You've knocked at the door to eternal life, it's wide open for you, but will remain *opened only to those who commit themselves and accept Jesus Christ as their Savior.* In the ***It's Not Rocket Science*** motif, you're on the launch pad. Final stop is **'*eternal Life.*'** Enjoy the packages you have been given; continue the 'walk with Christ.'

---

[149] Dunn, p. 457.

Righteousness

As Paul addresses *righteousness* in Romans, he indicates that living a righteous life is *a key matter to living one's life in faith*. God treats us as **righteous** if *we* in turn respond to the Gospel and Jesus Christ in faith.[150]

When we become righteous, we do not become God or Godlike. When turning from sin to a trust and belief in God through Jesus Christ, we are deemed righteous in the eyes of God, and to be righteous before God, we are also considered **justified** (a legal term meaning 'pardoned').

As John Witmer points out, 'righteousness' and 'justify' though seemingly unrelated in English, are related in Greek. 'Righteousness' is *dikaionunē* and 'justify' is *dikaioō*.

Paul used the noun "righteousness" many times in his epistles twenty-eight times in Romans alone (1:17; 3:21,22,25,26; 4:3,5,6, 9,11,13, 22; 5:17,21; 6:13,16,18-20; 8:10; 9:30; 10:3-6, 10:14:17). Paul also used the Greek verb fifteen times in Romans. To *justify* a person is to declare them forensically (legally) righteous. Being declared righteous does not mean you never sin. It means you *'legally stand forgiven'* because Jesus Christ has paid the debt for your sins with His blood dying on the cross. And anyone who is truly justified by faith in Jesus Christ is going to live in the spirit of that justification; hence, 'the just shall live by faith.'[151]

Paul directs many of his ideas and theology of righteousness to his fellow Jews and Israel as their nation. The heart of Paul's theology on justification was the dynamic interaction between the righteousness of God as God's saving action for all who believed, and righteousness of God as God's faithfulness to Israel, His chosen

---

[150] Stanley, *Life Principles Bible*, Romans 1:17.
[151] Kroll, *Romans, Righteousness in Christ*, p.47.

people. Paul took it for granted that God's righteousness was to be understood as God's activity in drawing individuals into and sustaining them within the relationship as the power of God for salvation.

With the relationship God had with Israel, Paul believed Israel a covenant partner with God. Even though Israel had turned or sometimes 'failed possibly in its worship of God,' God still counted the covenant partner as remaining in partnership, despite the latter's continued failure. But the covenant partner could hardly fail to be transformed by a living relationship with the life-giving God.[152]

The words *righteousness* and *justification* in this study seem to be closely related, but as mentioned in the first section of 'RIGHTOUSNESS,' in English the terms are not; in the Greek language and usage, they are. Understanding the relationship of the two terms can be confusing as put forth by Paul. In the next chapter on *justification* some clarity will be expanded-on and help with understanding.

---

[152] Dunn, *The Theology of Paul the Apostle*, p. 344.

Justification

In Romans 3:21-31, Paul gets to the message of his epistle to the Roman church: 'The only way one can be *justified* before God *is by faith* through Christ. The righteousness of God is imparted because of faith; justification is a gift through the *grace of God*.'[153] '*No one can boast of salvation by human works or by law keeping*. God can and will justify everyone who trusts in Him *by faith apart from works*.'[154] This passage from Romans and the excerpt from Kroll's book indicated Paul was writing his Roman letter for the benefit of the Jews in Rome and the Jewish nation. Paul was disappointed that the Jews did not adopt his theology of Christ.

Quoting directly from Woodrow Kroll's book, *Romans, Righteousness in Christ*, he uses an analogy I believe worthy of reprinting:

> 'Humans have dug themselves in so deep that only God can get us out. God must enter our world or else we will never enter God's world. In establishing guidelines for writers of tragedies, the Roman poet Horace in his *Ars Poetica (191)* said, "Do not bring a god onto the stage, unless the problem is one that deserves a god to solve the problem." The human predicament is not one that even Horace's god can solve; only Abraham's God can solve humanity's predicament.

Need the question be asked, 'Who or what authority can justify us greater than the one True God?' We have been declared righteous in His sight when we seek His *grace and righteousness*

---

[153] Stanley, *The Life Principles Bible*, Romans 3:21-31.
[154] Kroll, *Romans, Righteousness in Christ*, p. 47.

through faith in Jesus Christ. A man cannot be deemed pardoned by our legal system if he has committed a major sin; only God can forgive us of sin. Let's not forget this process, and gift, was ultimately bestowed on mankind through the death of His Son, Jesus Christ, who was nailed to a cross and shed His blood.

Those who want righteousness from God must find it *'through faith in Jesus Christ.'*[155] For those who worship other god figures (deists) such as Buddha and Allah, this will not make them righteous. Having a deist point of view is not the same as being righteous, and neither will the righteousness of the one True God be given to the deist.

Even though this righteousness is available for all, it is applied only to those who believe in Jesus Christ as Savior. The *conditional element* of the Gospel *is faith in Jesus Christ*. This righteousness is placed upon us as a shroud when by faith we receive Jesus Christ as Savior.

Righteousness is from God, through Jesus Christ, to all who believe that the sacrifice on the cross by the Son of Man is all God requires as payment for the penalty of sin. Martin Luther said, "this is the very center and kernel of the epistle and of all Scripture," and indeed it is.[156]

Through God's grace, He sees us as justified, and our sins are redeemed (bought back) through the blood of Christ.[157] No one ever mistook Jesus for anything but a leader, and yet He came to serve. In fact, He performed the ultimate sacrifice by giving His life as the atonement for our sins so that *we* might have eternal life. There is only one way to heaven, and that is through faith in Christ, and by acknowledging our sinfulness and need for forgiveness. Likewise, when *we lead*, it should be as He did – in humility as a servant. Not to glorify ourselves, but to exalt the One who saved us.[158] The

---

[155] Stanley, *Life Principles Bible,* 2 Corinthians 1:22-24; 2 Timothy 3:15.
[156] Kroll, *Roman, Righteousness in Christ*, p. 49.
[157] Stanley, Life Principles Bible, Matthew 20;28: 1 Corinthians 6:20; 1 Peter 1:18,19.
[158] Ibid. LIFE LESSONS, Matthew 20:28, p.1164.

gift of justification comes with no prior conditions having to be met – only the redemption that is in Christ. It is God who justifies those who have faith in Christ, and His only Son's sacrifice was necessary because the God of the past had not fully punished sin. God presented Christ as the atoning sacrifice, a propitiation to win the favor of believers.

One may ask, 'When we accept Christ as Savior and are justified in the eyes of God, do the laws of God no longer apply?' Paul had a ready answer, that being, 'It may never be!'

The laws of God, for Paul, were holy and because God now saves through faith and *not the deeds of the (Jewish) laws*, could one ask, 'do His laws no longer apply?' Again, Paul would have said 'no.' Faith in Christ is the only proper response to the law, for what the law could not do, *Christ alone*, can do.

While doing research, and talking to fellow Christians, there were some that did not have a grasp of the *righteousness – justification concept*. Many Christians felt unworthy in their own conception in God's sight, especially if baptized at a young age. This may be a hard subject for the *new* very young Christians to understand, and that's why it's imperative to 'try to' explain the concept instead of the standard, 'be a good boy or girl, and God will love you.' Of course, He does and will. We might start the conversation that 'baptism is the *first step* in their Christian life after they have accepted Christ as their Lord and savior, and it's the first step that should guarantee eternal life.

The next chapter on the *benefits of justification* could also be a great place to start. Go over each benefit putting them in your own words – my hope, new believers will understand what a wonderful decision they made; the most important decision they will ever make.

You've Been Justified Complete with the Benefits and Work Ahead of You

Through scripture St. Paul gives us many examples of 'justification by faith, and the benefits of being justified.' The following benefits are but a few, and it would be a great time to consider them, and let them soak in. Your new outlook on Christianity and life has and will change significantly. The primary work ahead of you is your *obedience* and *responsibility* to God, the Son of God and the Holy Spirit and working *towards sanctification, salvation and holiness.*

Your Benefits Package Via Justification

1. The **First Benefit** may not come right away. For me, it has grown over a period of many years. God was in control, and there were times of stumbling, but I, and you will come to a point in your life where there is an inner sense of *peace* - the number-one benefit is **Peace with God**. If you are obedient and responsible to your heavenly Father, a feeling of peace will encompass you like a warm blanket on a chilly night. A comforting sense of well-being that permeates your heart and mind.

    No one can say there will not be 'trials and tribulations;' those two points of possible contention are what Christians learn from. You may stop and ask, 'Why God' on occasion, but the answers will come – maybe not instantly, but the answers will come - through prayer.

    Through prayer, meditation, and reading your Bible, your peace with God will grow stronger. Your fellow Christians, friends, co-workers and all you interact will know there is something special and changing within you. If asked, or questioned, it may be perfect timing to share your testimony. Memorize Philippians 4:7: 'And the Peace of God which surpasses all understanding will guard your heart and minds in Jesus Christ.'[159]

2. The **Second Benefit** offers you a *Helper* – a mediator working in your behalf directly with God in none other than Jesus Christ. 'For there is one God, and *one mediator* also between God and men, the man and Son of God, Jesus Christ.'[160] When St. Paul writes there is one God, he is referencing the *'Shema'* – Israel's statement of faith.[161] As believers in Jesus Christ, Paul's foundational belief was not replaced; it was deepened. Jesus is not just another deity, but God Himself as mediator. God is the perfect listener, and if you stay quiet long enough in your quiet secluded space and pray *every day*, you will receive words of encouragement and wisdom we all need.

Another way to see Jesus as our mediator is that of a *defense attorney*. There is nothing we as believers can do in *our* world to mediate with God. Jesus represents those who have placed trust in Him. There is no mediator other than Jesus Christ if one wants access to God.

3. A **Third Benefit**. We are but mere mortals – humankind. God is Omnipotent (Almighty), and the day will come when we are all called to stand before Him. Many sermons are based on the questions: 'Are you ready to stand before God;' 'will you be left standing at the end of times;' 'do I have *a leg to stand on before God*?' If you have placed your trust and faith in Jesus Christ, the answer is 'yes!'

---

[159] Stanley, *Life Principles Bible*, Philippians 4:7.
[160] Stanley, *Life Principles Bible*, 1 Timothy 2:5.
[161] Ibid. Deuteronomy 6:4-9.

Because of Christ, not our own merit, we stand firmly in God's Love. Without Christ, you don't have a 'leg to stand on' in front of God; *Christ is our only access to God the Father.* 'Whether we like it or not, we are accountable for everything we do and say because at the judgement, every secret motivation, desire, and act will come out into the open. Are there undisclosed sins in your life? If Jesus is your Savior, you are forgiven for *all* your transgressions. He has removed the penalty of your sin and has left you spotless in return.[162] 'Nothing is secret that will not be revealed, not anything hidden that will not be known and come to light.'[163] Rest assured, you will be standing shoulder - to - shoulder with Christ on the day of judgement. This is the **Third Benefit** you can count on.

4. As believers, many pastors remind the congregations to *Rejoice in the Hope and Glory of God* – **a Fourth Benefit.** Having Hope in the Glory of God, whether you want and comprehend it, there will be big, positive changes in your life.

All will experience 'peaks and valleys' in their lives but will learn new ways to handle whatever life throws in their direction. When justified by God through Jesus Christ, your life is going to change. It may be in small increments, but in time, the whole world will start to look and feel different – a good feeling difference. If you hit an impasse in life and the burdens of your world seem to be holding you down, listen to what St. Paul writes in Roman 5:3- 5, 'And not only this, but we also exult in our tribulations, know that tribulation brings about perseverance; and perseverance, proven character- ***Hope***. Now Hope does not disappoint; because the love of God has been poured out

---

[162] Stanley, *Life Principles Bible,* LIFE LESSONS, Romans 2:16. P. 1340.
[163] Ibid. Luke 8:17.

in our hearts by the Holy Spirit who was given to us.'[164] Trials, difficulties, and adversities are often God's way of developing Christ-like character in us. No one likes trials, but the Lord can use them for our good, *if we will trust Him*.[165]

5. The tribulations of which Paul speaks result in ***'Patience,' a Fifth Benefit.*** This is not a passive quality, but the ability to remain strong while bearing the burden of tribulation.

   When passing through tribulations – spiritual, emotional, physical, or financial – it is God's Grace that will sustain and cause us to be steadfast. It is comforting to know that having been justified by faith, we can exult in our tribulations. Obey God and God's Love to them. In Romans 5:9-11,[166] Paul, puts forth the concept of leaving the consequences to God.[167] We tend to learn more in our valley experiences than on our mountain tops.[168]

6. Justification means ***'Encouraging Hope,' a Sixth Benefit***. 'This Hope does not disappoint because the Love of God has been poured out in our hearts and minds through the Holy Spirit that was given us.'[169] Biblical 'Hope' is not something we do at all (it's not a verb in the sense of 'hoping;' it's something we have by virtue of justification through Jesus Christ).

7. Justification means experiencing *The **Love of God***. The Hope we have in the Glory of God will prove to be genuine even though it may be tested in the cauldrons of tribulation.

---

[164] Ibid. Romans 5: 3-5.
[165] Ibid. *Life Principle Bible*, LIFE LESSONS, p.1344.
[166] Stanley, *Life Principles Bible*, Romans 5:9-11.
[167] Ibid. Exodus 19:5.
[168] Ibid. James 5:7-11.
[169] Ibid. Romans 5:5.

Why? Because the Love of God has been poured out within our hearts and is ***Another Benefit of Justification***. God's Love has been generously poured (Greek: *ekchumnō)* on us, not given grudgingly or halfhearted.

The word 'pour' is the one Jesus used when He said, 'This is my Blood of the Covenant, which is *poured out for many for forgiveness of sin*.'[170] God graciously and generously loved us when He justified us, and that Love is an everlasting Love, as strong today as it was then.[171]

The sacrifice of Christ on the cross arose out of the heart of God filled with the Love of God. All the blessings are ours because at some point in the past, without our help, we have been justified by God and are now being treated as if we are righteous. Thus, having been justified by faith, we have proof of the Love of God.

8. Justification includes the ***Gift of the Holy Spirit***.[172] This is the benefit of God's Love being poured into our hearts through the Holy Spirit. It is the Holy Spirit who pours into the hearts of believers a sense of what *will be* because God has justified us. He switches from the present to the future.

9. St. Paul lists still another benefit in these words: 'Having now been justified by His (Christ's) blood, ***we shall be saved from the wrath of God through Him***.' In addition to the blessings we presently enjoy due to justification, there is yet the promise that we will be saved from the 'wrath of God' through Christ.

When justified by the blood of Jesus, God removed His 'entire wrath' from our permanent record, from our present lives, and from our future. If we continually place our faith in God through Jesus Christ, *we will not be* subject

---

[170] Ibid. Matthew 26:27,28.
[171] Ibid. Jeremiah 31:3.
[172] Ibid. Romans 5:5.

to God's future wrath during the coming tribulation-end of days.[173] Nor will we be condemned to hell on the Judgment Day.[174]

When Jesus died in our place on the cross, He paid our debt and satisfied God's Holy demands against us.[175] Once the atonement was made, we were declared righteous in God's sight and were removed from under the heavy weight of God's wrath.[176] We've been reconciled to God,[177] and that exempted us from all future expressions of God's wrath.

10. *Justification means being saved by Christ's life.*[178] There is some confusion over this benefit derived from being justified. Paul said, 'For if while we were enemies, we were reconciled to God through the death of His Son, much more, having been reconciled, we shall be saved by His life.' The answer to the question, 'Are we saved by Christ's death, or are we saved by Christ's life?' The answer to both in 'yes!'

Ephesians 1:7 reads, 'In Him we have redemption through His Blood, the forgiveness of our sins, according to the riches of His Grace.'[179] 'Without shedding of blood, there is no forgiveness.'[180] Jesus had both to bleed and die to atone our sins. Our salvation came through Christ's death.

Today, Christ sits at the right hand of the Father interceding on our behalf.[181] *He is our 'Advocate with the Father.'* He is our great high priest, representing our

---

[173] Ibid. Thessalonians 1:10; 5:9.
[174] Ibid. Revelation 2:11-15.
[175] Ibid. Isaiah 53:10; Romans 5:8; 6:23.
[176] Ibid. Romans1:18.
[177] Ibid. Colossians 1:21,22.
[178] Ibid. Romans 5:10.
[179] Stanley, *Life Principles Bible,* Ephesians 1:7.
[180] Ibid. Hebrews 9:22.
[181] Ibid. Hebrews 7:25.

interests before God. The gift of Christ's atonement keeps on giving.[182]

11. ***Justification Means Continued Rejoicing.***[183] Do you ever think back about what your life was like before you were saved? How were you doing things, thinking about others, your relationships, were you happy? You may have had happiness, but was it coupled with Joy?

We make up for the absence of Joy with a presence of 'what we perceive will give a sense of Joy. We buy (spend money), we travel, some collect rare items, we 'network,' Facebook, some turn to drugs, but are these ways we may be desperately trying to find a sense of Joy. St. Paul's ***Final Benefit of Justification*** is once we have been reconciled to God, wrath departs, and ***Joy makes its entrance***.

The reason we can continue to rejoice in our lives is *we continue to be reconciled to God*. God's wrath has been appeased, therefore removed, and we are now on speaking terms with Him. This is what brought Joy in the first place. But since reconciliation continues to affect our lives, and always will, we continue to enjoy the reconciliation, rejoicing (a relationship that is strengthened and has been restored).

We've come to the end of the chapter on Paul's views of justification, the 'benefit package of justification that accompanies us in *our walk*ing in sanctification-to salvation; it began with the benefit of Peace and ends with Joy. I can think of no better combination and message for all – ***Peace and Joy.***

---

[182] Ibid. 1 John 2:1,2.
[183] Ibid. Romans 5:11.

Sanctification and Salvation

In Chapters 6 and 7 in the book of Romans, St. Paul begins his transition *from justification – to sanctification*. The subject of sanctification was not only addressed in Romans but in many of Paul' letters (Corinthians, Ephesians, Colossians, and others). In many cases studying the Bible there may have been only one verse that touched on sanctification; other epistles may have several.

Working "to become" and live more Christ-like is a lifetime journey: 'walking the walk,' step-by step, one theological idea building upon the former. Each step is interrelated and paying attention to each will help total understanding of sanctification.

> 'Once justified, *our journey into a spiritual life has just begun. *The Christian life (in Christ) is the walk from new birth to heaven, and that requires spiritual growth along the way. *Spiritual growth* is a process by which the Holy Spirit feeds us from God's Word, takes away sinful and childish attitudes, and conforms us more to the image *'in - Christ.'* We call the process **sanctification**.'[184]

Paul transitions smoothly between the discussion of justification in Chapter 5 to sanctification in Chapter 6 of Romans. Although there is a sharp contrast between the two, the intimacy of the relationship between justification and sanctification is clearly seen in the ways they are connected in the chapters. *Basically*, the contrast between the two is this:

- Justification deals with the penalty for sin,

---

[184] Kroll, *Romans, The Righteousness in Christ*, p. 87.

- Sanctification deals with the *'power of sin.'*

- Jesus as your Lord and Savior? By faith – and as is presented in Romans 5:1,[185] justification is a declarative act of God. 'Peace with God' is a fruit of oneness with Him. Before we trust Christ as our Savior, we are his enemies – hostile to Him because of our sin.[186] Yet on the Cross, Jesus justified us, which means He *declared* us not guilty of our transgressions. He clothed us in His righteousness and liberates us to have a deep, intimate relationship with Him. The enmity we had with God is abolished,[187] and we can have peace and unity with the Lord. We move from darkness to light, from enemies to beloved children, and from death to life.[188]

- As seen in Chapter 6, sanctification is a *progressive act* of God. Both deal with the sinner – justification with the *unsaved sinner*, and sanctification with the *saved sinner*.

- One result of justification is salvation; the results of sanctification and salvation should be *holiness*. Although distinctly different, justification and sanctification are flip sides of the one work of God saving humankind.[189]

'Therefore, as you have received Christ Jesus the Lord, *so, walk in and with Him*, having been firmly rooted and being built up in Him and established in your faith, just as you were instructed, and overflowing with gratitude.'[190]

---

[185] Stanley, *Life Principles Bible*, Romans 5:1.
[186] Ibid. Colossians 1:21,22.
[187] Ibid. Ephesians 2:13-16.
[188] Ibid. LIFE LESSONS, p.1344.
[189] Kroll, *Romans, the Righteousness of Christ*, pp. 89,90.
[190] Stanley, *Life Principles Bible*, Colossians 2:6,7.

How did you receive that is exactly how you grow into the maturity of sanctification – *by faith*.

The ability to accomplish all God has planned for you is with you through the presence, power, and wisdom of the Holy Spirit. So, if you wish to develop your relationship with Him and become all you were created to be, you must willingly surrender yourself to His promptings and trust Him, no matter what He commands you, do – 'so walk in Him.'[191] 'Everything that exists was created by Him and for Him. It is all under His authority including all the nations, governments, and rulers of the earth. Of course, some people disagree with that by not acknowledging the Lordship of Christ. But their opinion is irrelevant because one day 'at the name of Jesus every knee should bow, of those in heaven, and of those on earth, and those under the earth (Philippians 2:10).'[192]

Remember, God knew you before you were born, during your mortal life, and afterlife. God will not put you in situations or predicaments that He does not know the outcome.

It is notable how in Romans 6, Paul draws immediate ethical corollaries for being 'in Christ.' The conclusion of the paragraph that elaborates the 'with Christ' motif (Romans 6:1-11) is: 'So also you must reckon yourselves dead indeed to sin and alive in God in Jesus Christ.'[193] And the application follows at once in Romans 6:12-14:

> 'Therefore, do not let sin rule in your mortal body to obey its desires, and do not give sin control of what you are or do, as weapons of unrighteousness. But give God decisive control of yourselves as being alive from the dead and of what you are and do, as weapons of righteousness. For sin shall not exercise

---

[191] Ibid. Colossians 2:6,10,11.
[192] Ibid. LIFE LESSONS, Colossians 2:10, p. 1440.
[193] Ibid. Romans 6:11.

lordship over you; for you are not under the law but under grace.'[194]

'Each one of us has a legal sin debt that *must* be reconciled. Yet none of us can pay it because of our sin nature. So, Christ knowing every sin we would ever commit, took our record of wrongs upon Himself and wiped them all out with His own blood. Our sins were cancelled forever. No one can ever condemn us because our Savior, the Lord Jesus Christ, paid the penalty in full.'[195]

Sanctification and your being 'in Christ' *is not* a mystical-cosmic removal from the real world. On the contrary, it becomes a starting point, base camp, *'a launching pad'* for a quite differently motivated and directed life.[196] The secret of sanctification is not found in a sanctimonious formula or a deeper mental experience with the Lord. The 'secret' is found in three words:

- Know (Romans 6:3)
- Consider (Romans 6:3)
- Present (Romans 6:13)

Be especially aware of the principles as we seek to understand the relationship between justification and sanctification. To live a sanctified and holy life after we are saved and squelch the desires to continue to sin, we much adhere to these three principles.[197]

Principal 1: The Need to Know (Romans 6:3-5)

To the Apostle Paul, knowledge of why we deserved condemnation is the foundation for sanctification. And knowledge of what happened to us when we were justified is essential to understand sanctification, therefore sanctification is built on knowledge, *not on feelings.*

---

[194] Stanley, *Life Principles Bible*, Romans 6:12-14.
[195] Ibid. LIFE LESSONS, Colossians 2:14.
[196] Dunn, *The Theology of Paul the Apostle*, p. 411.
[197] Kroll, *The Righteousness of Christ*, p. 90.

To show the immaturity of those who would continue to sin after justification so that *'grace may abound,'* Paul introduces the sacrament of baptism as evidence that a life of unrestrained, unrepentant sinful behavior *cannot coexist with death to sin*. Paul states we should know that 'all of us who have been baptized in Christ Jesus have been baptized in His death.'[198] Baptism into Christ means *to be incorporated into Him*, to become a member of His body,[199] and to share with Him those experiences that were historically His, but are vicariously ours (His crucifixion, death, burial and resurrection).

We are buried with Him by baptism into death. Burial with Christ signifies that sin no longer judicially has a hold on us. The ordinance of Christian baptism beautifully portrays this burial into Christ in which the old order of a death-controlled life comes to an end and the new order of a Christ-controlled life begins.

When a Christian has been symbolically raised from the dead from the waters of baptism, even as Christ was raised from His Jerusalem grave, the purpose of that Christian's resurrection is he or she should walk in newness of life. Hence, we enter in His life and become a part of Him spiritually, yielding to Him our desires, our wishes, ourselves.[200]

At the Cross of Calvary, a victory was won that provided the believer with the power not to live as he or she once did, serving the 'old master' (sin), but to live eternally serving a new master (Christ).

F. F. Bruce refers to this truth as stated in Galatians 2:20 and then continues:[201]

> 'Similarly, in Galatians 6:15, Paul speaks of "the cross of our Lord Jesus Christ, but which the world

---

[198] Stanley, *Life Principles Bible*, Romans 6:3.
[199] Ibid. 1 Corinthians 12:13
[200] Kroll, *The Righteousness of Christ*, pp. 90-91.
[201] F.F. Bruce, *The Epistle of Paul to the Romans*, (Grand Rapids, MI: Eerdmans, 1963), Galatians 2:20

has been crucified (perfect tense) to me, and I to the world." In these two passages from Galatians the perfect tense denotes a present state produced by the past event of Romans 6:6.' [202]

Moreover in Galatians 6:14 there is 'probably' a side glance at an alternative meaning of the verb *crucify* (*stauroō*), namely *"fence -off,"* so that Paul's words also imply, "that cross forms a permanent barrier between the world and me, and between me and the world,' from the old man (sin) in Colossians 3:9[203] and Ephesians.[204] He (the old man) belongs to the "present evil age" from which the death of Christ delivers his people.[205]

"Knowing that Christ, having been raised from the dead, is never to die again; death no longer is master over him."[206] This is the third time the word *know* in one of its forms has appeared in the first nine verse of this chapter in Romans on sanctification. It should be increasingly evident that the sanctified life begins with the informed mind, not with inspired emotions.

St. Paul had no doubt that Jesus was alive. He had beaten death, and because He would never die again, He was master over death, not the other way around. Justification is a completed transaction by which we have once and for all passed into the resurrection life of our Lord. Jesus Christ can never die again. After we die with Him to sin, we never die to sin again. Death has no more dominion over Him and no more dominion over us.

Therefore, the foundation of sanctification is *knowing* what Christ has already accomplished for us though His death - the starting point of realizing that we are Holy in Him. To live a

---

[202] Stanley, *Life Principles B*ible, Romans 6:6.
[203] Ibid. Colossians 3:9.
[204] Ibid. Ephesians 4:22.
[205] Ibid. Galatians 1:4.
[206] Ibid. Romans 6:9,10.

sanctified and Holy life after we are saved, we also must *now* adhere to the second principle.[207]

Principle 2: Consider Yourself Dead

Understanding the first principle as a process of sanctification is knowing what had been given us on our behalf at Calvary. It is but the first principle in the process of sanctification.

St. Paul couples to the first principle a second. "Even so consider yourselves to be dead to sin, but alive in God in Christ Jesus."[208] In the story of Abraham, Abraham believed in and believed God without question. Therefore, it was reckoned (Greek: *logizomai*) or credited to him as righteous. We also saw this word in Romans 5:12, for until the law sin was in the world, but sin is not imputed (*logizomai*) when there is no law. As a reminder, the word means to credit something to the account of another. As F.F. Bruce writes:

> 'This "reckoning" is no vain experience but one which is morally fruitful, because the Holy Spirit has come to make effective in believers what Christ has done for them, and to enable them to become in daily experience, as far as may be in the present conditions of mortality, what they already are "in Christ" and what they will fully be in the resurrection life.'[209]

When we daily count ourselves to be dead to the penalty of sin and alive in God, there should be no temptation to continue to sin. We will refuse the temptation out of thankfulness to God for counting us and treating us as righteous. To live a sanctified and holy life after we are saved and squelch the desire to continue in sin, we must adhere to yet a third principle.

---

[207] Kroll, The Righteousness in Christ, p. 93.
[208] Ibid. Romans 6:11.
[209] Bruce, *The Epistle of Paul to the Romans*, p. 139.

Principle 3: Present Yourself to God (Romans 6:13)

The third and final principle in living a sanctified life is stated negatively:

> "Do not go on presenting the members of your body to sin as instruments of unrighteousness; but present yourselves to God as those alive from the dead, and your members as instruments of righteousness to God."[210] When Paul talks of 'instruments,' the Greek translation and word (*hoplon*) means weapons or arms of warfare.

Paul uses the same Greek word in 2 Corinthians 10:3,4: "For though we walk in the flesh, we do not war according to the flesh, for the weapons of our warfare are not of the flesh." Knowing what Christ accomplished for us in the past resulted in our justification and considering or reckoning ourselves dead to the penalty of sin because we have been justified, we are now to keep our weapons from being given to sinful purposes. 'It is extremely important to understand that though we do not yet have our glorified bodies and still live in tents of flesh, we are involved in a real spiritual battle, and the enemy's goal is our destruction. The devil does everything he can to undermine our faith and impede our progress in God's will by putting temptations in our pathways that appeal to our fleshy desires. Yet because the Spirit of the living God dwells within us, we can serve Him wholeheartedly in faith and win this war through obedience.[211]

Paul is stating, "Do not keep on continually presenting your members as instruments of unrighteousness." In other words, once you have been justified, there is no place, or reason for you to continue to do the things you did (sin) before you were justified. You cannot continue living in adulterous relationships after you

---

[210] Stanley, *Life Principles Bible*, Romans 6:13
[211] Ibid. LIFE LESSONS 2 Corinthians 10:3,4, p.1393.

are saved. Lying, cheating, stealing, coveting are sins not to be repeated. What has happened in the past, stays in the past.

Once we have been justified, we present ourselves to God, and while the fruit of that presentation continues day by day, we do not repeat the process day by day. There comes a point in a believer's life (at salvation) when he or she must decide to live for God and abandon habits of the past. If one who claims to be a Christian does not exhibit that kind of commitment to God, there is every reason to question whether that person has experienced salvation.[212]

Paul's concept of sanctification, then, is not a daily dying to one's self. It is being mature enough to rest wholly on the finished work of Calvary, knowing we have been justified there, daily reckoning work to be finished and constantly presenting ourselves to be used by God.[213]

As William Barclay wrote, "Christianity can never be only an experience of the secret place; it must be a life in the market place."[214] When we as believers are obedient to these commands, we find ourselves on a road (pathway) climbing progressively toward the resurrection life of the Lord. The Lord has a promise for those who seek sanctification in this manner: "Sin shall not be master over you." That is the good news![215]

I have come to believe that many Christians get baptized, and 'that's it - they believe they're saved for eternity.' They 'get stuck in an 'eschatological tension' and continue to live their lives as before – some in the fast lane, some continuing to sin as much as ever before; others, *my hope is you*, get to the right pathway to sanctification and salvation.'

It's always an ongoing journey in our mortal lives. Another common thread was *the term obedience to God*. When we leave 'this

---

[212] Kroll, *Romans, The Righteousness of Christ,* p. 94.
[213] Ibid. p. 95.
[214] William Barclay, *The Letter to the Romans* (Philadelphia: Westminster, 1957). p. 87.
[215] Kroll, *Romans the Righteousness of Christ,* p. 95.

world, all have an audience' before God and His Son.

Sanctification is a subject that is peculiarly relevant in the present day. Strange doctrines have risen lately upon the whole subject of sanctification. Some doctrines appear to confound it with justification. Others fritter it away to nothing, under the presence of zeal for free grace, and practically neglect their sanctification all together. Others are so afraid of works being made a part of sanctification, they hardly find any place for works in their lives, churches and religion.

Others set up a wrong standard of sanctification and fail to attain it, waste their lives in repeated secessions (jumping) from church to church in the vain hope that they will find what they want. In our present day, a close examination of the subject as a great leading doctrine of the gospel, may be of great use and give peace within our souls.

Sanctification is the inward spiritual work the Lord Jesus Christ works in mankind by the Holy Spirit when He calls them to be true believers. He not only washes them from their sins in His own blood, but He also separates them from their naturel love of sin in their current world. Christ puts a new principle in our hearts and helps us to become 'Christ-like' in life.

The instrument by which the Spirit affects this work is the 'Word of God,' though He sometimes uses afflictions and providential visitation "without the Word."[216] The subject of this work of Christ by His Spirit is called in scripture a "sanctified" man.

Christ has undertaken everything that his people's souls require, not only to deliver them from the guilt of their sins by His atoning death, but from the dominion of their sins, by placing in their hearts the Holy Spirit; not only to justify them, but to sanctify them. 'He is, thus, not only their righteousness but the sanctification and redemption.'[217]

---

[216] Stanley, *Life Principles Bible*, 2 Peter 3:1,2.
[217] Ibid. 1 Corinthians 1:30.

Christ "has reconciled 'you' in the body of His flesh through death, to present you holy and unblameable and unreproveable in His sight" (John 17:19; Ephesians 5:25,26; Titus 2:14; 1 Peter 2:24; Colossians 1:22).[218] 'The idea that Christianity is merely a social club and that believers have no responsibility other that believing in God absolutely contradicts scripture. We are to be zealously pursuing the work the Lord has called us to do[219] motivated by faith and hope in Him and committed to serving others and leading them into a growing relationship with Jesus Christ. We are also to grow deeper in our love and devotion to Him through prayer and Bible Study so that we will obey, glorify and please Him always.'[220] From these verses we find Christ undertakes the sanctification, no less than the justification, of all his believing people.

Both are alike provided for in that "everlasting covenant ordered in all things and sure, of which the Mediator is Christ." In fact, Christ in one verse is call "He who sanctifies, and His people are sanctified."[221] [222]

Leslie Courtney in *Brief Thoughts on Sanctification* uses an analogy of a "most beautiful mosaic art piece" that has been covered by dirt and filth. 'You can see bits and pieces of the beautiful image, but you cannot quite make out what it is due to all the grime caked on it.

This is how it is with humanity. There are still bits and pieces of the divine image that are seen in mankind, such as when we love one another and do good thing for the betterment of all humanity. Still, there is a lot more dirt and filth that can be seen in our race.

> "Basically, in the process of sanctification, God becomes like a person intent on restoring that

---

[218] Ibid. John 17:19; Ephesians 5:25,26; Titus 2:14; 1 Peter 2:24: Colossians 1:22.
[219] Ibid. Ephesians 2:10.
[220] Stanley, Life Principles Bible, LIFE LESSONS, Titus 2:14, p. 1480.
[221] *Are We Sanctified*, http://www.gracegems.org/Ryle/ho2htm.
[222] Stanley, *Life Principles Bible*, Hebrews 2:11-13.

beautiful mosaic to its former beauty. God begins to wash that mosaic, cleaning off the dirt, grime, and filth, until we finally start to see the beautiful image that lies underneath. He even retouches the faded colors and adds touches that were not there to begin with! He does this because He desires to see that beautiful image restored to its former glory.'"[223]

---

[223] Leslie Courtney, *Brief Thoughts on Sanctification, Leslie Courtney-Memoirs of a Rogue Scholar*. http://www.lesliecourtney.com/2013/05/29/brief-thoughts-on-sanctification.

The Lord's Supper

In contrast to the difficulties in deriving the theology of the Lord's Supper from other religions in that time, there is little difficulty in deriving the early Christian meal practice from within its own tradition. Fellowship meals were a feature of both Pharisees and Essenes. Jesus's own practice of table fellowship was criticized for its disregard for the appropriate limits. The sensitivities on this score are evident also in Luke's careful telling of the story of Peter and Cornelius,[224] as well as in the 'incident at Antioch.'[225] They directly illumine the concerns addressed by Paul both in 1 Corinthians 8:10[226] and Romans 14:1-3.[227]

Paul records the tradition authorizing the Lord's Supper as the account of the last supper of Jesus with His disciples, which Paul himself received and passed on to the Corinthians at the foundation of their church.[228] A comparison of this tradition with its variant versions is instructive. The material peculiar to Matthew and Mark in the following version in scripture as compared to Paul's version:

> 'He took bread, blessed, and broke it and gave it to them and said, "Take, eat, this is My Body." Then He took the cup, and when He had given thanks and gave it to them, and they all drank from it. He said to them, "This is My blood of the new covenant which is shed for many."'[229]

---

[224] Stanley, *Life Principles Bible*, Acts 10: 9-16.
[225] Ibid. Galatians 2:11-14.
[226] Ibid. 1 Corinthians 8:10.
[227] Ibid. Romans 14:1-3.
[228] Ibid. 1 Corinthians 11:23-29.
[229] Ibid. Mark 14:22-24: Matthew 26:26-28.

Paul's version in Corinthians:

> 'For I received from the Lord that which I also delivered to you: that the Lord Jesus on the same night in which He was to be betrayed took bread; and when he had given thanks, He broke it and said, "Take, eat; this is My Body which is broken for you; do this in remembrance of Me." In the same manner He also took the cup after supper, saying, "This cup is the new covenant in My blood. This do as often as you drink it, in remembrance of Me."
> 'For as often as you eat this bread and drink this cup, you proclaim the Lord's death till He comes.'[230]

'The Lord's Supper not only looks back at Christ's sacrifice and gives Him praise for His great gift of salvation, but it also looks ahead to the day when we will see Him again and enjoy our Heavenly home with Him forever.'[231]

Modern theologians believe the Paul/Luke version of the Lord's Supper is the closer of the two. Paul's version shows a further elaboration at the end –'"Do this as often as you drink it, in remembrance of Me, For as often as you eat this bread and drink from the cup, you proclaim the death of the Lord until He Comes."' There need be little doubt, Paul did indeed derive his founding tradition of the Last Supper from common tradition, and nothing Paul says in 1 Corinthians 11:23-26 counts against the view that the tradition itself stemmed ultimately from the event known as the Last Supper itself.

The most striking and challenging feature of Paul's theology of the Last Supper is undoubtedly his further understanding of the church as also the 'body of Christ.' Paul's language here has provided the basis for all subsequent theological reflection on the correlation between sacrament and church, between the one body

---

[230] Stanley, *Life Principles Bible,* 1 Corinthians 11: 23-26.
[231] Ibid. LIFE LESSONS, 1 Corinthians 11:26, p. 1374.

that is the bread, and the one body that is the church. It is more important that we pay close attention to the language Paul used,

> 'The cup of blessing which we bless, is it not the communion of the blood of Christ? The bread which we break, is it not the communion sharing of the Body of Christ? For we, *though* many, are one bread *and* one body; for we all partake of that one bread.'[232]

> 'This is my body for you.' 1 Corinthians 11:24

> 'Therefore, whoever eats of the bread or drinks the cup of the Lord in unworthy manner will be guilty of the body and blood of the Lord.'[233] 'For he who eats and drinks in an unworthy manner eats and drinks judgment to himself, not discerning the Lord's body.'[234]

In the above passages in this letter to the Corinthians, if anyone disregarded the sanctity of the bread and cup, he or she was putting the Corinthian church in deadly peril. Paul's concern centered on the bread and the cup as the primary expressions of the unity of the congregation and as means to that unity when properly celebrated.

Paul's Theology and Christology of the Lord's Supper

In 1 Corinthians 10:4[235] Paul identifies Christ 'typologically' (the study and interpretation of types and symbols, originally, especially in the Bible) or spiritually with *the rock from which*

---

[232] Stanley, *Life Principles Bible*, 1 Corinthians 10: 16,17.
[233] Ibid. 1 Corinthians 11:27.
[234] Ibid. 1 Corinthians 11:29.
[235] Ibid. 1 Corinthians 10:4.

drinking water was given to Israel in the wilderness.[236] Paul does not hesitate to use that traditional episode to present Christ as the source (*the spiritual rock*) of the 'spiritual drink.' But he makes no attempt to identify Christ as the source of *'spiritual food'* itself (contrast 1 Corinthians 10:16,17).[237] He was evidently content to use 'link points' given him by his traditions versus trying to force a point upon them. Presumably 'spiritual' has the same sort of ambiguity as in the preceding reference.[238]

We need simply mention again, that Paul identifies the blessed cup and the broken bread as a sharing in the 'blood of Christ and the body of Christ.' And we should not forget that all the 'body talk: (the embodiment) has in mind the body of Christ. The point of the Lord's Supper is to feed and sustain the relation with Christ, precisely as a communal/corporate relationship.'

Any move in Eucharistic practice to isolated celebration (as the Lord's Supper was intended simply to feed the individual with spiritual food) or that detracts from it as a shared experience runs counter to Paul's emphasis and detracts from his Christology of the 'body of Christ.'

The table of the shared meal is the 'table of the Lord.'[239] He is the host at the meal. We recall that it was the exclusiveness of the loyalty that the Lord was seen to require,[240] that marked out 'the church of God'[241] so sharply from pagan cults.

1 Corinthians 11:23-26, underlines the direct continuity between Jesus's hosting the Last Supper and the shared meals that were such an important event of the early churches. Despite the long history of dispute about the character of Christ's presence in the celebration of the Lord's Supper, exegetically the meaning of 'this is My Body' is as open and ambiguous as the talk of 'spiritual food.'

---

[236] Ibid. Exodus 17:6
[237] Ibid. 1 Corinthians 10:16:17.
[238] Stanley, Life Principles Bible, 1 Corinthians 10:3,4.
[239] Ibid. 1 Corinthians 10:21
[240] Ibid. 1 Corinthians 10: 21,22
[241] Ibid. 1 Corinthians 10:21-22, 32.

The traditions of Jesus and from Jesus form a vital component in the celebration of the here-and now relationship with Christ. Even if word gatherings and meal gatherings were separate, it is clear enough that the element of word/tradition with the shared bread and the wine together constituted the sacrament from the beginning.

The Pauline additions to the traditional wording constitute the Lord's Supper as an occasion that forms a high point in time from which the congregations can look both backward and forward – back to its crucial foundational event and forward to its anticipated consummation.

The precise meaning of the twice repeated 'in remembrance of Me' continues to occasion debate. But it certainly cannot be reduced merely to an invitation to a pious remembering on the part of those who eat the bread and drink the cup. The point seems rather to constitute the shared eating and drinking of what Jesus Himself consecrated as symbols of His death as itself and the act of remembrance, "the praise filled representation of that which happened … *once and for all.*"[242]

The second addition, "for as often as you eat this bread and drink the cup, you proclaim the death of the Lord until He comes," points just as firmly forward. In effect, here Paul makes the Lord's Supper the cord that binds the already – not yet tensioned together and keeps it from falling apart. Or alternatively expressed, the Lord's Supper is presented here as a kind of bridge by which believers (again, not so much individually but precisely as the Body of Christ) cross through the sometimes-raging torrents of the eschatological tension.

The alternate which Paul does not hesitate to formulate, is his oft-repeated warning that grace willfully refused brings judgment in its train.[243] Such blatant disregard for the denial of the "for you" of Christ's death can only be maintained by a deliberate closing of

---

[242] Dunn, *The Theology of Paul the Apostle*, p.622.
[243] Stanley, *Life Principles Bible,* 1 Corinthians 11:27-32.

the 'eye and ear' to the "for you" responsibility of the well-to-do members of the congregation for the others.

Thus, to abuse the Lord's Supper is to invite the Lord's judgment. Here, as in all such matters, discernment is required. It is only by recognizing such differences between the Lord's Supper as it should not be celebrated and the Lord's Supper as it should be celebrated that they could avoid being condemned.

To accept such a rebuke would transfer the judgment of the Lord from condemnation to discipling. In all this, the Lord, whose death was represented in their common participation in the bread and the cup, was also the Lord over the meal (the Lord's Table, the Lord's Supper). Woe to those who forgot the latter in abusing the former.

'By linking the Lord's Supper with judgment as well as spiritual food, with Christ's coming again as well as His death, Paul underlines the extent to which celebration of the Lord's Supper does indeed "proclaim" the whole gospel and provide instruction as well as sustenance during the long slog from the already to the not yet.'[244]

The Lord's Supper is celebrated across all Protestant religious denominations. It is a sacrament that reminds us Christ died for our sins and was resurrected. It is celebrated most often on the first Sabbath of the calendar month. Looking back to the first Lord's Supper sacraments, I knew they were special, but didn't know why. I do remember our pastor always ended the celebration with the following statement: "It's a backwards look at the Cross, and a forward look to the Crown. This due in Remembrance of Me." Indeed, it is – Amen.

---

[244] Dunn, The Theology of Paul the Apostle, pp. 621-623.

Martin Luther – A Fresh Look at the Old Doctrine of Justification by Faith

Sometime between 1515 and 1516, Martin Luther made the great discovery from which the 'Reformation' was born. Luther discovered, or had the revelation as to what *is* 'Justification by Faith' – the doctrine that has been at the heart of Protestant theology since. It is not too much to claim that his 'new theology' decisively transformed European Christianity, and with it, European history, theology, political thought, and culture. It was the doctrine of *'justification by faith'* that led to Luther's secession from the Church of Rome, and from church leaders and princes being forced to take sides for or against the Reformation with all the consequences that followed. What proved to be so important and had such a radical impact?

Until the time of Luther's 'new theology,' he had been a devoted monk (of the Augustinian order), a gifted student, a devoted teacher of the Bible. He earned his doctorate in 1512.

A personal internal problem bore discord in his spiritual life. He had no peace of heart, no quietness of conscience. The doctrine of human sinfulness depressed him and no amount of *penance,* (a sacrament in which a member of the church confesses sins to a priest and is given absolution – often at a price) nor confessions seemed to remove his own sense of guilt before God.

What Luther feared most of all was *'the justice of God.'* He understood the anger and judgment of God against sinners (the wrath of God). During that time period, when life was often very short, the thought of death could be very frightening, for after death came the judgment, and for the guilty, hell loomed as a terrifying prospect and future for life after death.

But then came the great discovery as he wrestled with the

words of St. Paul's letter to the Christians in Rome. The 'sticking point' for Luther was Paul's talk of the *justice of God* as revealed in the Gospel.[245] How could God's 'just punishment of sinners be gospel, that is "good news" (the gospel mentioned in Romans is the Gospel of Jesus Christ)?'

Let's let Luther tell his own story:

> "I greatly longed to understand St. Paul's Epistle to the Romans, and nothing stood in the way but that one expression, 'the justice of God,' because I took it to mean the justice whereby God is just and deals justly in punishing the unjust. My situation was that, although an impeccable monk, I stood before God as a sinner troubled in conscience, and I had no confidence that my merit would please Him. Therefore, I did not love a 'just and angry God,' but rather hated and murmured against Him. Yet, I clung to the dear Paul and had a great yearning to know what he meant.
>
> Night and day, I pondered until I saw the connection between the justice of God and the statement that 'the just shall live by faith' (Romans 1:17). Then I grasped that the justice of God is that righteousness by which through grace and sheer mercy, *God justifies us through faith*. Thereupon I felt myself to be reborn and to have gone through open doors into paradise. The whole of Scripture took on a new meaning, and whereas before the 'justice of God' had filled me with hate, now it became to me inexpressibly sweet in greater love. This passage of Paul became to me a gate to heaven."[246]

---

[245] Stanley, *Life Principles Bible*, Romans 1:17.
[246] Taken from Roland Bainton's, *Here I Stand* (London: Hodder & Stoughton, 1951), p. 65, (slightly adapted).

What was Luther's great discovery? How did he interpret 'Justification by Faith?' There was obviously a crucial shift in his understanding of God. It involved a shift from talk of *God's justice to talk of God's justifying*.

It is important to recognize that the language in the following is the language of *court law*. Luther's problem was the medieval church's emphasis on God and Christ as *'a judge.'* The whole of life on earth was but a preparation for the final court of judgment, presided over by the judge of all the world that would settle where each person spent eternity. There is no shortage of such talk in the Bible to feed such fears. We need only to reference the following passages:

- Matthew 25:31-46,
- Mark 9:43-48,
- Romans 2:5-10
- 2 Corinthians 5:10.

The assumption then, was wherever the New Testament spoke of God's justice, it was God's verdict against sin and His sentence against the sinner that was in view. For anyone with an 'unquiet conscience, Bible reading on God's justice was a fearful experience.' Luther's revelation was two-fold. First, it was when Paul writes about God justifying, he had in mind not so much God's condemnation of sin *but His acquittal of the sinner*. The distinctive feature of the Gospel is not what it says about God's justice in passing a sentence on human wickedness. Rather, the distinctive feature is what the Gospel says about God *pardoning the wicked*. The judge can also pronounce a verdict of *'not guilty.'*

Second, it was that the court law metaphor could not be pressed, as though it was the only way of picturing God's attitude of His human creation. God was not only Judge, but also Father and as in family-relationships are not governed solely by strict rules, as though a judge continued to act only as a judge even in his own home and with his own. God is also kind and generous to His children. He accepts them as they are, with all their faults and failings – He welcomes the sinner, warts and all.

What Luther realized was of tremendous importance – that *God's acceptance is the beginning of spiritual striving, not its goal.* The light that dawned on Luther was Christianity is not a matter of anxious striving for God's favor. It is not to be thought of as a dogged discipline in hope of winning God's final commendation.

Instead, Christianity starts from the recognition that we can *never work* for our passage to heaven. This is not because we could not succeed if we did try, but because reliance on our own efforts turns us away from God. Christianity starts from the amazing discovery that "God justifies the ungodly."[247] He is the God who offers to accept the wicked as they are and starts renewing them from that point.

This was a tremendously powerful grasp of the Christian Gospel. No wonder it lit the fires of the Reformation in sixteen-century Europe. For countless thousands terrified of the prospect of hell, dismayed by the thought of purgatory, and put off by the abuses of the medieval Church, it was *good news* indeed. Christianity starts from the offer of God's unconditional grace; an offer extended to all who accept Jesus Christ as Savior through faith – all ages, stages, or condition"[248]

---

[247] Stanley, *Life Principles Bible*, Romans 4:5.
[248] Dunn and Suggate, *The Justice of God: A Fresh Look at the Old Doctrine of Justification by Faith* (Grand Rapids, MI: William B. Eerdmans Publishing Company), pp. 5-8

The Fruit of the spirit

"But the Fruit of the Spirit is love, joy, peace, long suffering, kindness, goodness, faithfulness, gentleness, self-control.

Against such there is no Law.

And those *who* are Christ's have crucified the flesh with its passions and desires. If we live in the Spirit, let us walk in the Spirit."[249]

When we are in union with Christ, the Holy Spirit's primary responsibility is to produce His likeness in us. He teaches us how to be totally dependent upon God, which produces love, joy, peace patience, kindness, goodness, faithfulness, gentleness, and self-control in us. We cannot genuinely produce these qualities on our own because our sinfulness mars them. However, when we are completely reliant upon the Lord and obey the promptings of His Spirit, they flow from us freely and draw other people to Him.

Everyone who belongs to Christ has died with the Savior on the Cross. That means we have given up our right to dictate the course of our lives, because we realize that fleshly inclinations only lead to disappointment and ruin.[250] We turn our lives over to the Lord because only He can lead us in the very best path possible.'[251]

'Believers who truly walk in the Spirit radiate integrity. They do not hide their true feelings, harbor self-serving intentions, nor would they ever try to take advantage of you. In fact, you may

---

[249] Stanley, *Life Principles Bible*, Galatians 5:22-25.
[250] Ibid. Proverbs 14:12.
[251] Ibid. LIFE LESSONS, Galatians 5:22-25, p. 1410.

feel as if you can trust them with your most intimate secrets. You may even find yourself *opening-up* to them in a way that is quite uncharacteristic of you.'

Spirit filled believers do not pretend to be perfect. In fact, they often offer humble apologies before they are confronted with wrongdoing because the Spirit alerts them when they have offended or hurt someone. Secure in their relationship with the Lord and their worth in Him, they respond quickly once that realize and admit their sin or error in judgment. They remember that the Holy Spirit is continually sanctifying – transforming them into the image of Christ. Therefore, they are not discouraged but are thankful His grace is always available to them when they stumble and that He is teaching them to rise above the fleshly appetites and desires.

Specifically, their lives exude nine virtues: love, joy, peace, patience, kindness, goodness, faithfulness, gentleness, and self-control. This fruit is not simply a mark of the Spirit-filled life, it is the preeminent evidence of a life in Jesus Christ.

When reading about God's gift of grace, ask Him to show you how you can be more grace-filled with others. He may help you recall the unkind things you've done in the past, but when you surrender your will to Him, He will make you a kinder person who reflects His love to many.

The fruit of the Spirit *isn't produced* when we focus on ourselves; it is a result of being singularly centered on Christ.[252] These virtues are goals we can pursue, and they were never intended to demonstrate our dedication and resolve because *you and I cannot yield fruit.* Rather, the Holy Spirit is the producer and we are merely the bearers. And the harvest that results from our walk with Him merely reveals our dependency on and sensitivity to His promptings.[253]

AMEN

---

[252] Stanley, Life Principles Bible, John 15:5.
[253] Ibid. *Life Principles Bible,* ANSWERS TO LIFE'S QUESTIONS, 'What is the fruit of Spirit and how does it grow in me?', Galatians 5:22,23, p.1409.

Words & Definitions

Anthropology: The study of humankind, including the comparative studies of societies and culture.

Ecclesiology: The study of churches, theology as applied t h e nature and structure of the Christian Church.

Embodiment: A tangible or visible form of an idea or quality; for quality instance, Sue was the embodiment of beauty.

Eschatology: The study of the last things, or events in a present age or time. The word is used to cover such important events as the second coming of Christ (Parousia), the judgment of the world, the resurrection of the dead, and the creation of a new heaven and earth with emphasis on the events leading up to the 'main events'.

Eschatological Tension: Those events which may have included strife, danger, differing ideas or philosophies, etc. leading up to the main event, of a specific event at a specific time.

Exegesis: A critical explanation or interpretation of a text or portion of a text, especially in the Bible.

Linguistic Distinctiveness: The study of human speech including the units, nature, structure, and modification of language; a capability of making a segment of utterance different in meaning as well as in sound from an otherwise-identical utterance.

Omnipotent: In reference to **God**. Almighty or infinite in power, having very great (infinite) authority.

Omnipresent: The omnipresent *God*. Present everywhere at the same time.

Omniscient: The Omniscient *God.* Having complete or unlimited (infinite) awareness or understanding, perception of all things.

Ontology: A branch of metaphysics (philosophy, especially in its more abstruse branches; the underlying principles of a subject or field of inquiry; a treatise (4th century BC) by Aristotle dealing with first principles, the relation of universals to particulars, and the 'teleological doctrine' of causation [the philosophical doctrine that final causes, design and purpose exist in nature].

Soteriology Theology: The doctrine of salvation through Jesus Christ.

Bibliography

Alexander the Great, www.jewishhistory.org/alexander_the great, accessed Sept. 9, 2019.

America .... A Godless Nation, *Salvation in Jesus Ministry,* www.sijministry,YOUTUBE, accessed Sept. 1, 2019.

Are We Sanctified? http://www.graceage.org/Ryle/hO2.

Bainton, Roland, *Here I Stand.* London: Hodder & Staughton, 1951.

Barrett, David, Christopher D. Hudson, and Todd Bolen, *Bible Atlas and Companion.* Urichsville, OH: Barbour Publishing.

Barton, Bruce B., DMin, Philip W. Comfort, DLit, Phil Kent Keller MDiv, Linda Chaffee Taylor, and David R. Verrman, DDiv. *Life Applications, Bible, Commentary, Ephesians,* Carol Stream, IL: Tyndale House Publishers, 1996.

Borg, Marcus J., and John Dominic Crossman, *The First Paul, Reclaiming the Radical Visionary Behind the Church's Conservative Icon.* New York: Harper Collins Publishers, 2009.

Briggs, C.W. *The Apostle Paul in Arabia.* Ballston, NY. JSTOR: *The Biblical World* 41, no. 4 (April 1913), 255-59.

Brittle, Irving L. Jr., *St. Paul the Apostle: The Right Man at the Right Time.* Sheridan, WY, 2020. Penhouse, LLC.

Bruce, F.F., *The Epistle of St. Paul the Apostle,* Grand Rapids, MI: Eerdmans Publishing Co., 1963

Bruce, F. F., *Paul: Apostle of the Heart Set Free.* Carlisle Cubrian CA3,OQS UK: Paternoster Press LTD, 1977.

Callewaert, Joseph M., *The World of St. Paul the Apostle.* San Francisco, CA: IGNATIUS Press, 2-11.

Cole, Dan P., *Corinth and Ephesus, Why Did Paul Spend Half His Journeys In These Cities.* Biblical Archaeology Society (BAS), BR 4.06, Dec. 1968.

Concise Oxford English Dictionary. Oxford University Press: 2012.

Courtney, Leslie. *Brief Thoughts on Sanctification, Leslie Courtney- Memoirs of a Rogue Scholar.* http://www.lesliecourtney.com/2013/05/29/brief-thoughts-on sanctification.

Dockery, David S., General Editor. *Concise Bible Commentary.* Nashville, TN: B & H Publishing, 1998, 2010.

Dunn, James D. G. *The New Perspective on Paul, Revised Edition,* Grand Rapids, MI: William B. Eerdmans Publishing Co, 1989.

Dunn, James D. G. *The Theology of Paul the Apostle.* Grand Rapids, MI: William B. Eerdmans Publishing Co., 2006.

Dunn, James D. G. and Alan M. Suggate, *The Justice of God.* Grand Rapids, MI: William B. Eerdmans Publishing Co., 1993.

En.wikipedia.org/PaultheApostle.Biblical Narratives,Early Life, accessed September 14, 2019.

Fairchild, Mark R., *Why Perga? Paul's Perilous Passage Through Pisidia.* Biblical Archaeology Society (BAS Library), BAR 39:06, Nov./Dec. 2013.

Furnish, Victor Paul, *Corinth in Paul's Time: What Can Archeology Tell Us?* Biblical Archaeology Society (BAS Library), BAR 14:03, May/June,1998.

Griffith-Jones, Robin., *The Gospel According to Paul.* New York: Harper Collins Publishers, 2004.

Harvey, Hannah B. *The Art of Storytelling: From Parents to Professionals The Great Courses.* Chantilly, VA: The Teaching Company, 2013.

Ironside, H. A., *An Ironside Expository Commentary, 1 & 2 Corinthians.*
Grand Rapids, MI: Kregel Publications, 2006.

Ironside, H. A., *An Ironside Expository Commentary, Romans and Galatians.* Grand Rapid, MI: Kregel Publications, 2006.

Kennedy, D. James, *Evangelism Explosion,* Fourth Edition, Carol Stream, IL: Tyndale House, 1996.

Kroll, Woodrow, *The Book of Romans: Righteousness in Christ,* Chattanooga, TN: AMG Publishing, 2002.

Lea, Thomas D., and David Alan Black, *The New Testament: Its Background and Message,* 2nd Edition, Nashville, TN: B & H Academic, 2003.

Lockyer, Herbert, *All the Apostles of the Bible,* Grand Rapids, MI: Zondervan, 1972.

Maccabean Revolt – *Wikipedia*, en.wikipedia.org/wiki/Maccabean Revolt, accessed September 14, 2019.

Mack, Burton L., *Who Wrote the Bible.* New York: Harper Collins Publishing, 1995.

Mandino, Og, *The Greatest Salesman in the World.* Hollywood, FL: Bantam Books, Published by Arrangement with Frederick Fell, Inc., 1968.

Mandino, Og, *The Greatest Salesman in the World, Part II, The End of the Story.* New York: Bantam Books, 1989.

McGee, Dr. J. Vernon, *Thru-the Bible Commentary Series, The Epistles, Romans Chapters 1-8 & 9-16.* Nashville, TN: Thomas Nelson, 1991.

McGrath, Alister, and J. I. Packer, *ROMANS Hodge.* Wheaton, IL: Crossways Books, 1993.

Mendals, Doran, *Why Paul Went West: The Difference Between the Jewish Diasporas.* Biblical Archaeology Society (BAS Library), BAR 37:01, Jan./Feb. 2011.

Moore, Beth, *Portraits of Devotion.* Nashville, TN: B & H Publishing Company, 2014.

Murphy-O'Conner, Jerome, *On the Road and On the Seas with St. Paul: Sidebar: The Second Missionary Journey of St. Paul.* Biblical Archaeology Society, BR 1:02, Summer 1985.

Murphy-O'Conner, Jerome, *What Was Paul Doing in Arabia.* Biblical Archaeology Society (BAS Library), BR 10:05, Oct. 1994.

NIV Study Bible, Grand Rapids, MI: Zondervan Publishing, 2011.

Paul, David J. *Defending the Faith, Catholic Teaching on Justification and Sanctification,* 1996. http://www.efpeople.org/apologetics/page51a037.html.

Phillips, John. *The John Phillips Commentary Series-Exploring Romans.*
Grand Rapids, MI: Kregel Publications, 1969.

Platt, David. *Radical, Taking Back Your Dream from American Dream.* Colorado Springs, CO: Multnomah Books, 2010.

Stanley, Dr. Charles F., *God Has a Plan for Your Life.* Nashville, TN: Thomas Nelson Publishing, 2008.

Stanley, Dr. Charles F., *The Life Principles Bible.* New American Standard Bible. La Hubra, CA: Thomas Nelson, 2009.

Stanley, Dr. Charles F., *I Am Saved – Now What?* InTouch Ministries, Atlanta, Georgia. September 9, 2015.

Tabor, James D., *Paul and Jesus: How the Apostle Transformed Christianity.* New York: Simon and Schuster, 2012.

Walker, Margaret (editor), Robert Bronder (designer), Dorthy Resig (managing editor), Susan Laden (publisher, Washington, DC). *Paul: Jewish Law and Early Christianity,* ebook, Biblical Archaeology Society (BAR), 2012,

Whiston, William, trans., *The Works of Josephus.* Peabody, MA; Hendrickson Publishing, 1987.

Willis, Gary., *What Paul Meant.* New York: W.W. Norton & Company, 1997.

Wilson, A. N., *Paul: The Mind of the Apostle.* New York: W.W. Norton & Company, 1997.

Wright, N. T., *Paul for Everyone: The Prison Letters, Ephesians, Philippians, Colossians, and Philemon.* Louisville, KY; Westminster John Knox Press, 2002.

Wright, N.T., *Paul and the Faithfulness of God, Parts I & II,* Minneapolis, MN; Fortress Press, 2013.

Wright, Tom, *Paul for Everyone: Romans: Part One, Chapters 1-8.* Louisville, KY: Westminster John Knox Press, 2004.

www.gotquestions.org/Olivet_discourse.htmp. As of Sept. 4, 2019.

www.ingramcontent.com/pod-product-compliance
Lightning Source LLC
LaVergne TN
LVHW040157080526
838202LV00042B/3194